Never a Dull Moment

MARY E. HEATON

Russian Hill Press Book
United States • United Kingdom • Australia

R
H
P Russian Hill Press

The names and details concerning some people in *Never a Dull Moment* have been changed. The author has on a few occasions changed the order of events, where those changes benefit narrative flow without altering a factual telling of the story. Otherwise all dialogue and events took place as the author remembers and recounts them in these pages.

ISBN: 978-1-7351763-6-9 (softcover)
ISBN: 978-1-7351763-7-6 (eBook)
Library of Congress Control Number: 2020821437

Cover designed by Christine McCall

Acknowledgments

I would first like to thank my editor, Violet Moore. Six years ago, after I wrote my first book, *Rambling Through the Emerald Isle*, she said to me, "Mary, when you write you next book . . ."

I was so taken aback by her words I said, "Violet, you think I am going to write another book, really?"

"Certainly," she said. I will never forget her words and of course I had to live up to them. Thank you for believing in me, Violet.

A huge thank you to my long-time girlfriend, Cris Cassell, for reading and pre-editing my memoir. I have known her for forty-three years and she knows most of my attributes, but even she discovered new elements while reading my manuscript. Cris has been teaching English composition and drama for over twenty-seven years at the Academy of Arts College in San Francisco. I respect her expertise and feedback. She has been a great help to me for both of my books.

I would also like to thank my newfound cousin, Hilda Berlinguette, who contacted me through 23andme, noticing we shared a surname on our profiles. I took out my family tree and discovered we share the same great-great-grandparents, Anders and Karin Lindstrom, from Sweden. Hilda and I made an instant connection and have much in common.

I also want to thank Hilda's husband, Roger for reading my manuscript. I felt it would be beneficial to get a man's perspective about my memoir. I appreciate both for taking the time to read my stories and giving me feedback. They were both very supportive of me moving forward with my book.

I want to thank my Dad and Mom and my six siblings, Coll, Peg, Pat, Katy, Chris, Mark, and Aunt Jane, for molding me into the person I am today. Without them I would not be me.

And lastly, to my husband Duane, and children, Alana, Amando, Colton, Samuel, and Jillian. Thank you for all the love, support and material from which I wrote my stories. I love you all.

the war and used them as slave labor to work in their mines throughout Japan, Thailand, and Manchuria during World War II.

One fateful day during my father's imprisonment, he was so weak after working all day in the icy mine that he collapsed on the two-mile trek back to the barracks. He did not have one ounce of strength left to carry on. His lifeblood sapped from his very bones as he lay on the path, snow collected on his dirty, tattered clothes. From a distance, it looked as though a heap of rags in the middle of the trail. My father's decimated ninety-pound body afflicted with scurvy and beriberi, lay in a frigid makeshift grave, where he believed he was going to die. He closed his eyes, welcoming death, which would be a comfort. As he lay in between this world and the next, he felt gentle hands shaking him, calling to him from what seemed like another world. "Are you alive? Hey buddy, wake up!"

My father heard but was slow to respond. His thoughts as he lay semiconscious in the snow, do I want to live? No, I want to sleep, to die.

Then God whispered into my father's ear, "It is not your time, my son." A flicker of warmth began to burn in my father's heart, and he began to stir. He chose to live.

My father murmured, "I'm alive." My father's savior was a mere man who still had strength left in his body. He picked my father up and carried him back to camp to the infirmary.

He gave my father some water to drink and left before my father could thank him. A pine box was placed underneath my father's cot by a Japanese guard because my father was not expected to live.

Richard C. Hansen shocked everyone when he did survive. Later, after he regained some strength, he made inquiries to find out who this extraordinary man was that had saved his life so he could properly thank him. My father found out from the other prisoners that the man's name was Jesus B. Gutierrez or "Jimmy" as everyone called him around camp. My father found Jimmy and simply thanked him for saving his life by shaking his hand.

Where is this angel, this man, Jesus B. Gutierrez, who had the compassion to stop and save my father's life? I want to thank him for his humanity, for helping a fellow human being in need. I want to tell him that he also is responsible for the lives of my brothers and sisters and me because, without his random act of kindness, we wouldn't have been born. Dear Jesus, you will never be forgotten wherever you are.

On August 15, 1945, several months after Jesus saved my father's life, Japanese Emperor Hirohito announced the surrender of Imperial Japan to the United States. Then, on September 2nd the surrender document was signed on board the U.S.S. Missouri by Foreign Affairs Minister Mamoru Shigemitsu.

The following week the United States Naval

hospital ship, *Rescue*, began picking up 6,212 war prisoners from Japan and took them to Guam. They arrived on September 23rd, my father's twenty-sixth birthday. The most serious cases stayed aboard the *Rescue*, my father being one of them, and continued to San Francisco for further treatment. My father was in the hospital for a total of eight months. After he arrived in San Francisco, he was able to call his mother, Hulda Hansen, and when she answered the phone and heard her youngest son's voice, she fainted. She had been told in May of 1942 that her son was missing in action. She and my father's siblings assumed he was dead.

Epilogue

After I wrote "My Father's Angel," I couldn't stop thinking about Jesus B. Gutierrez, the man who saved my father's life. I wanted to find him and thank him myself. So, with the help of military records I found online, I set forth on a mission to find this extraordinary man.

I first found Jesus's military serial number on a website for WWII prisoners of war. With this in hand, I was able to access records on Ancestry.com, which I am a member. I was able to find where Jesus was born in Deming, New Mexico, on September 25, 1921. With this, I was able to find out that he had died three years after my father, on July 16, 2000, and is buried at Fort Bliss National Cemetery in Texas. I was amazed to find out Jesus not only served in WWII but also served in the Korean and Viet Nam Wars. After all he endured in a prison camp in Japan, he kept serving his country. This man was quite exceptional.

I found Jesus's family tree on Ancestry.com. I saw on his family tree that Jesus had a son, so I sent an email to the person who owns the account for Ancestry.com, a John Lopez. He is a cousin of Jesus Gutierrez. I was able to share the story about my father with John and told him what an honorable man his cousin Jesus was. I saw on the family tree that Jesus married Katherine Biehl on August 26, 1952, and they had a son named Raymond. I asked John if he could get ahold of his cousin's son so I could thank him. John informed me that Mr. Gutierrez's son, Raymond had died, but that Jesus's sister Josie was still alive at the age of 95. John told me the next time he goes to visit his cousin Josie, he would tell her how her brother, Jesus, had saved my father's life in a prison camp.

I thanked John for his kindness. I felt elated that I was able to get to know a little bit about the man who saved my father's life. And in a roundabout way, I was able to thank Jesus by retelling the miraculous story of him saving my father's life to his relative, John. I believe my father would be proud that I did all that I could to find his angel and fellow prisoner. If I ever find myself in Fort Bliss, Texas, I will place flowers on Jesus B. Gutierrez's grave in his honor.

My wish came true on Thanksgiving Day in 2013, by way of my daughter, Alana. She was visiting El Paso where her boyfriend Tommy's parents live. I asked them to buy flowers and go to Fort Bliss cemetery to visit Jesus's grave. They told me they would be honored to do the task for me.

Alana placed flowers on Jesus's grave and thanked him for saving her grandfather's life. She also thanked him for her life and mine. Alana sent me two photos on that Thanksgiving Day, and I wept tears of gratitude to her, Jesus, and my father.

Alana at Jesus B. Gutierrez's grave in Texas.

My Mother Kathleen

Kathleen Caffy

Her grandparents came by ship from the
Emerald Isle.
Named after her mother but answered to
Colleen.
Her Papa loved her dearly, made her smile.
Her love for music was very keen.
The second daughter of three had the bluest
eyes.
Chubby as a cherub angel, a towhead
became a dark-haired beauty that caused
sighs.
Many fond admirers but used her head.
Graduated early to become a nurse.
Moved to Manhattan for nursing school.
Gave her blood to get money for her purse.
Cheerful, always singing, breaks a rule.
Graduates in three years with her class.
Irish Colleen faithfully goes to Mass.

Godmother

Mary Elizabeth Sweeney was born in the state of Maryland on December 8, 1921. Her grandparents were immigrants from Ireland. She lived in a poor household with her brother John, sister Ann, and her parents. Mary grew up during the depression, and she knew what it was like to "live without."

Mary blossomed into a beautiful young woman. She was five feet, seven inches tall, with wavy brunette hair, light blue eyes, and a great figure. Many young men were attracted to her, but she married Robert Browne at the young age of nineteen. They had gone to grade school together and Robert was tall, dark, and handsome.

They had a happy first year of marriage, but in 1941, when WWII broke out, Robert joined the Navy and was sent to the Pacific. Mary was alone and occupied her time working at a local department store. One day while Robert was away, Mary was crossing the street on her way to work and was hit by a car. She suffered internal injuries and had to stay in the hospital for a few weeks. She was lonely and scared.

When Robert came home from the war in 1945, he was a changed man. He was thin and nervous, constantly smoking cigarettes. Mary didn't understand the change in him. She desperately wanted to have a child. After several years of not getting pregnant, Mary saw a specialist. He told her that the injuries she sustained from the car accident had left her uterus scarred and unable to sustain a pregnancy. Mary was devastated.

Mary and Robert moved to Oakland, California, where he was stationed at Treasure Island. They moved to an apartment building on Rand Avenue and became good friends with their neighbors, my parents, Kate and Dick Hansen. When the Korean War broke out in 1950, my father and Robert went to sea. Mary and Mom were inseparable. Mom had just given birth to my sister Colleen and Mary was a big help to her, but most of all they kept each other company.

After years of being childless, Mary and Robert decided to adopt and in 1955, they adopted a two-year-old boy and named him Bobby. My mom had given birth to my sister, Peggy, in 1951 and my brother, Patrick, in 1954. My dad was transferred to San Diego where Katy was born in 1956, but the two families stayed in touch.

My father retired from the Navy in 1959 and moved the family back to Northern California, settling in San Lorenzo. He was hired at the Lawrence Livermore Laboratory, where ironically Robert already worked. The Brownes had moved to Livermore in 1957 and tried to talk my parents into moving there too. Chris was born in 1959, Mark in 1961, and I in 1962. The three of us were born at Oak Knoll Naval hospital, which sadly was torn down. My mother asked Robert and Mary to be my godparents, and I am also her namesake.

In 1966 after seven years of commuting to Livermore, my dad decided it was time to move. My parents bought a house three blocks from the Brownes. I grew up having Thanksgiving and Christmas with them.

Mary was 41 years old when I was born. As a child, she seemed so old to me. She chain-smoked and drank a lot of beer. There was a lot of drama when Mary was around. She was always complaining about the food my mom cooked or that our house was messy. One Thanksgiving she started to cough while she was eating and Robert gave her the Heimlich maneuver and she threw up on the dining room table in front of all of us.

Mary was a perfectionist and was a difficult person to be around. She was an extremely negative person. She and my mom talked on the phone forever, even though they lived down the street from one another. They never walked to each other's houses. That amazed me. They only lived three blocks apart, but when they did see one another, they always drove.

I found out in my twenties that Robert had had an affair with a secretary at the lab. Mary would not divorce him because of her Catholic faith, but I don't think she ever forgave him. After Bobby left home, Mary moved into her own room. Robert and Mary constantly bickered.

It was sad because after Bobby got married,

he moved to Santa Rosa and rarely came down to visit his parents. His wife and Mom did not get along. The last fifteen years of Mary's life, she and Bobby were estranged.

Mary became a hypochondriac. There was always something wrong with her or so she said. She was constantly going to the doctor, but he never found anything wrong. She was constantly taking over the counter medication for her "ailments" and eventually she did get sick. Her kidneys shut down from all the medication she took, and she eventually lost a kidney. She died in 1997 at the age of 76.

Even with her eccentric behavior, I still loved Mary. At times, she was so funny. I believe she loved me like the daughter she never had. Mary was very generous and always gave me gifts at Christmas and for my birthday. I think my brothers and sisters were envious because all their godparents lived far away and they never received gifts from them. When my parents went away together, I stayed with Mary and Robert. I loved to hear the stories about her growing up in Maryland.

Mary viewed the world with her glass half-empty. But as I look back at all the stories she told me about her life, I can see why. Life had been very difficult for her. It's too bad that it affected her so adversely. I am glad that my mother and she became friends and gave comfort to one another over the years. I am happy to know she is finally at peace.

Kids, We Almost Lost Your Sister

Mark, Mary, and Chris

I have been told this story many times by several of my siblings, but I only have a few memories of it myself. When I was three years old, I had an accident in the backyard of our San Lorenzo home. When I was young I was given the nickname Mimi by my parents because whenever I wanted to go somewhere with my siblings, I would yell me, me. Only five people called me Mimi: my dad, mom, Aunt Jane, Mary, and Robert.

We had a Doughboy pool in our backyard. It was about three feet high, and several metal rods reinforced the sides of the pool. As the story goes, I picked up one of the metal rods, and my brother Mark tried to take it away from me. But as any young person would do, I ran away from my brother not wanting him to take it.

As I was running, I tripped over a rock and I fell to the ground. When I did not move, Mark ran into the house to get my parents. When my mother and father came out of the house, they saw me laying on the lawn. As they came closer, they could see the metal rod coming out of my head and through my blonde curls. My mom was in shock, shrieking. My father ran over to me to assess the damage. He thought I was dead.

He gently picked me up and could see that the rod had not gone through my skull, but it had pierced through the skin of my cheek. My mother was relieved to see that it had not killed me. They brought me into the kitchen, and my dad put me on the Formica counter.

Dad said, "Mimi, hold very still. I am going to pull this rod out of your mouth." My dad carefully pulled the rod out of my mouth, and my mother put gauze on the outside of my cheek, pressing down to stop the blood flow.

They took me to Oak Knoll Hospital in Oakland. I remember seeing the doctor in his green scrubs. He said, "You are a very lucky little girl. Mouth wounds heal quickly. You do not need stitches. All you need is a butterfly bandage and you can go home."

My parents were quite relieved, but I think I gave them a few gray hairs that day. I came very close to death and my parents knew it. So when my dad used to tell the story he always began with, "Kids, we almost lost your sister that day."

Mom and Mary

My earliest memories are of sounds, specifically, obnoxious ones. Piercing sounds terrified me to the point where my mother was on constant alert to protect me from any earsplitting sound in the near vicinity.

My first memory of a scary sound was when I was three years old. A whistle blew at noon in San Lorenzo, near the Mervyn's department store where my mom loved to shop. She brought my brother, Mark, and me with her while my five siblings were in school. Mom kept track of the time on her watch, and a minute before the clock struck twelve, she covered my ears tightly with her white-gloved hands. If she didn't do it in time and I was exposed to the screeching of the whistle, I would scream in terror.

We lived close to the Hayward and Oakland airports during my first four years of life. I have memories of wailing while jets flew low overhead. Mark and I enjoyed playing on the swing set in our backyard, but if a jet or plane came in his sights, Mark would run over to me and clamp his hands over my ears to protect me from the rumble of the engines.

My poor family had to put up with my howling every time a fire truck or ambulance whizzed by our house. I know it wasn't easy for them, but I couldn't help it. I had extremely sensitive hearing and still do. When I became a mother myself, my children marveled at how I could hear what they were up to in any part of the house, especially if I was in my bedroom while they were getting cookies out of the kitchen cupboard. I always joked about how I had bionic hearing like Lindsay Wagner in *The Bionic Woman,* which happened to be one of my favorite TV shows when I was a kid.

I believe my acute sense of hearing led me to connect with quiet hobbies such as sewing, gardening, yoga, swimming, painting, reading, and writing. I steer clear of loud machines, casinos, and video games. When my children got invited to birthday parties at Chuck E. Cheese or Boomers, I asked my husband to take them. Being in loud environments with flashing lights and dinging machines gives me sensory overload and causes me stress and anxiety. I also abhor lakes where speedboats or jet skis are present. I avoid NASCAR and Monster Truck shows.

In contrast, I delight in the sounds of nature. I find pleasure in walking, sailing, and watching birds flit through the sky. I relish the sound of the wind whooshing through the trees while sitting on the deck of my cabin in the Sierra Nevada Mountains near Yosemite. I love the soft call of the mourning doves, the buzzing of hummingbirds as they whiz by me, off to find nectar in brilliant wildflowers. I am transfixed by the human-like sounds that come from the ravens as they flap through the woods, and the rapid knocking of the woodpeckers.

It is in nature where I listen to the whispers of my ancestors giving me ideas for stories or an answer to a problem. It is in the stillness of the early morning, as the sun wakes the birds, when I gain the most insight. I open my eyes and lie in bed listening to the excited chirping of the wild birds as they begin their day, and it brings me joy.

Reflection

One of my earliest memories was looking at my reflection in a three-way mirror. I was shopping with my mom and my brother, Mark, at Mervyn's department store in San Lorenzo, California. The year was 1965 and I was three years old and he was four. I remember it so clearly because the person in the mirror looking back at me was terrifying. I hid behind my brother because I didn't want to look at myself. I was so ugly.

The day before, Mark and I were playing with two girls from our neighborhood, Julie and Pam. We had a swing set in our backyard, and children loved to come and play with us at our house. It was a warm, sunny spring day and our cherry tree was full of blush pink blossoms. The Scotch Broom plants that lined the redwood fence were in full bloom with their brilliant yellow flowers. Mark and Julie were on the two swings and trying to swing as high as they could. They were older and it was easier for them to swing. Pam and I were three, so the teeter-totter was better for us.

We sat on seats opposite from one another, holding the handles in front of our small bodies. The seats were metal and painted red. We could look at each other's smiling faces while we pushed on the teeter-totter. We were having a wonderful time until I fell off my seat. I fell hard on my bottom in the dirt. Pam was still in her seat and the momentum of the teeter-totter was still going when it hit me in the eye. The plastic caps that covered the metal tubes that the seat was welded on had come off, and the full end of the exposed metal tube hit me on my left eye. As it hit me, I fell back, my head hitting the ground.

By this time I was crying, and my brother Mark jumped off his swing and ran into the house to get our mom. Julie hopped off her swing and came over to comfort me. I screamed in pain by then. Pam was so upset, she started to cry, too, and our picture-perfect day came to an end and chaos ensued. My mom came running out of the house with Mark in tow. My mom was a nurse, so she was great in an emergency. Julie and Pam had disappeared. My mother scooped me up and brushed the dirt off my blue jumper and carried me into the house. She gently sat me on the Formica counter and began to assess the damage on my face.

My left eye had started to swell. She got a clean washcloth from the drawer and ran it under the faucet to get it wet. She very carefully wiped my dirty face and said, "Well Mimi, you aren't bleeding." I was relieved. Mark stood by, as our mother attended to me, his face scrunched with worry. Mom pulled a gray rubber ice pack from the cabinet. She went to the freezer and took out a silver metal tray of ice and twisted the metal grate to release the ice cubes. She put one piece of ice at a time into the ice pack. Then she screwed on the round lid and held it against my eye. She said, "Now Mimi, hold this pack on your eye. It will keep the swelling down."

My mom carried me to the couch in the living room and told me to stay lying down and to keep holding the ice pack on my eye. Mark sat with me for a little while, but he soon became bored and ran outside to find out where Julie and Pam had gone. I soon fell fast asleep from all the commotion that had transpired the hour before.

My two older brothers and three sisters arrived home at different intervals and asked mom what had happened to me. She told them about the accident and they each came over one by one asking me how I was and then eventually went about their business. My father came home from work at 5:45 p.m. and saw me lying on the couch watching TV. He walked over and picked me up and said, "What happened, Mimi?' I proceeded to tell him the tale. He gave me a hug and said. "You'll be fine by tomorrow."

The next day, my older brothers and sisters left for school before I got up. I think I slept in because of all the energy I expended the day before. I woke up and I could not see out of my left eye. It had swollen shut. I walked around the house calling for my mom and found her in the kitchen, washing dishes. "Mom, what's wrong with my eye, I can't open it."

My mother looked startled. She said, "It's okay Mimi. You will be able to see out of it tomorrow. Your eyelid is swollen," she said masking her emotion. She said, "We need to go shopping at Mervyn's. Please get dressed."

So I went into my room, put on a flowered T-shirt and green stretch pants. I came out to the kitchen and mom gave me a bowl of Cheerios to eat.

Mark had come in from the backyard and took one look at me and said, "What happened to Mary's eye?"

Mom said, "Marky, Mimi's eye is fine. Don't stare. It's not polite. Please, both of you get in the car. We need to go shopping." We hopped into the front seat of our bright red Chevy station wagon, and we were happily on our way.

We arrived ten minutes later at the Mervyn's parking lot. We got out of the car and Mom held one of my hands and one of Mark's. We entered the store, and I could see people staring at me in an odd way. I loved the smell of Mervyn's, that rubbery smell of new shoes. I loved looking at all the beautiful new clothes and jewelry, so I forgot about the people looking at me. We went to the ladies dresses. Mom needed to pick out a dress for a party she was going to the following week. I was walked around touching all the beautifully colored dresses when I came across a three-way mirror. I stood and looked at myself and I began to cry. "Mommy, what happened to me? I am so ugly!" My left eye protruded from my face. It was purple and blue and disgusting. It downright scared me. I felt like I was watching a scary movie and I was the monster. "Mommy, am I going to look like this forever?" I whined.

"No, you won't Mimi. In about a week, it will be gone," she said comfortingly. "Now, come away from the mirror."

I have to say that my mom was a consummate actress. She could always put on a happy face and not let you know how bad things were. I guess she did it to spare our feelings and to survive being a mother of seven children.

Christmas 1966

Mark, Chris, and Mary

I t was December of 1966 and Christmas was quickly approaching. I couldn't wait until Santa came to visit our house. I was four and a half years old and felt the excitement of the season tickling my tummy.

My family and I had moved into a new house in Livermore. The living room had a vaulted ceiling, so we purchased a Christmas tree that was eight feet tall, which seemed enormous to me. I couldn't wait to decorate the tree, but my oldest sister, Colleen, was in charge and she made the rest of us siblings put on ornaments and tinsel in an orderly manner. My brothers, Mark and Chris, ages five and seven, also wanted to help with the tree, but we had to abide by Colleen's strict instructions: Do not clump the tinsel.

Colleen is a perfectionist and we had to listen to her, otherwise, we couldn't decorate the tree. I watched her carefully take one strand of tinsel at a time out of the box and hang it precisely on the end of each branch, making sure it hung straight down, to look like an icicle. I tried my best to copy her, but I was too exhausted, so I finally gave up putting on tinsel and switched to ornaments instead.

Our new house felt like a mansion compared to our old one in San Lorenzo. We moved from a small, three-bedroom, two-bath house, to a four-bedroom, two and a half bath house, with a full basement. What a treat.

In our old house, we four girls were in one bedroom and my three brothers in another. My parents had the smallest bedroom since there were only two of them. My dad built triple bunk beds for my sisters and brothers. My sister, Colleen, the oldest, slept in a rollaway bed. When we moved into our new house, we only had to share a bedroom with one sibling, except for my oldest brother, Pat, who got the basement to himself.

I slept upstairs in our new four-level house with my sister, Katy, who was ten years old. Christmas Eve finally arrived, and I went to bed bursting with anticipation. Katy and I chatted for a while, and she convinced me that Santa and his reindeer were on the roof because she could hear tiny hooves prancing around on the shingles. I finally fell asleep and the night seemed to fly by like Santa's sleigh.

NEVER A DULL MOMENT

Mark and Chris woke us up with their frantic taps on our door. It was still dark, and I asked Katy what time it was, and she told me it was five-thirty in the morning. Chris knocked on my parent's bedroom door. Mom and Dad walked out of their room groggily, with dark circles under their eyes and frowns on their faces. I could hear my dad say a few bad words under his breath.

My sister, Peggy, who was fifteen at the time, took my hand and slowly led me down the two flights of stairs to the kitchen where I beheld a wondrous sight. There before me were five brand new Schwinn bicycles, each one a different color of the rainbow. Mine was a candy apple red tricycle with white handgrips and tassels. Mark's bike was a plum, two-wheeled bike, with training wheels. Chris had gotten a chartreuse Stingray bike with a black banana seat. Katy had gotten a metallic royal blue two-wheeler, and Pat had received a burgundy two-wheeler. It was just like being in a bicycle shop where the bikes are all lined up in a perfect row just waiting to be purchased by a parent for their fortunate child. I blinked my eyes again. This time it was in my house, and I was the lucky kid.

After the shock of seeing all the bikes wore off a little, I wandered into the living room and I could see presents on every surface. I felt completely overwhelmed, not knowing what to look at first. I had never seen so many gifts in any of my four years. With seven kids in our family, we had never gotten this much at Christmas. But this year, there really had to be a Santa.

I walked over to the hearth and there was a dollhouse with little plastic furniture, for me. My mom called my name and told me to look on the couch. I did, and there was a baby doll. She was beautiful, with blonde hair and blue eyes that closed when she was lying down and opened when I picked her up and looked at her face. I was ecstatic. I was the last child born to my family, so I never got to hold a baby, and here was a doll that looked like a real infant to me. Right then and there I named her Sleepy. She was all mine to love and take care of and dress.

I will never forget the magic of that Christmas and the wonder I felt. I found out years later that "Santa" was my Grandmother Claffy who left a small inheritance when she died. The money also helped to purchase our new house. What a gift my grandmother gave to our entire family.

Adventure with Chris

Mary, Mark, Chris, and Katy

When I was five years old, I went on an adventure with my brother, Chris, who was three years older than me. He was always up to mischief and felt the sting of our Dad's belt more than any of my other five siblings put together. Chris was curious by nature and had to figure things out for himself rather than learn from other people's mistakes.

One blazing summer afternoon in 1967, I saw my brother rummaging through the shelves in our garage, looking for something. I said, "Chris, whatcha lookin' for?"

"A big jar. Do you know where one is, Mare?"

"Yeah, there's one over there in the corner,"

I said, pointing my index finger in the direction of the jar. Chris went over and picked up an enormous glass jar that used to contain mayonnaise. My mom bought everything in large quantities at the Naval Commissary to feed our family of nine. I followed Chris into the kitchen where he opened a cupboard door and pulled out a box of striped plastic straws.

"Chris, whatcha doin'?" I asked.

"I am going to catch some black widow spiders."

"Can I come too?" I had three brothers and was used to catching lizards, insects, and snakes.

"Sure, why not. We need to walk down to Murrieta Boulevard, though. Do you want to walk that far? You are gonna have to keep up with me."

"Yes, I can do it. I want to go, Chris. Please?"

"Okay, Mare, let's go." He handed me the box of straws and he picked up the jar and wrapped his arms around it, holding it tightly.

Off we trotted down Norfolk Road to Pine Street and around the corner to Murrieta Boulevard. A cinderblock fence ran down the street until Portola Avenue. Concrete decorations were mounted in the middle of each section of fencing. Chris walked up to one and set the huge glass jar on the sidewalk. He pulled a straw out of the box I held in my hand and stuck it inside one of the holes in the decoration, on the concrete fence. He fished around inside the hole for several seconds and pulled out a black widow spider hanging from the tip of the straw. The spider was black like a fancy leather shoe and had two little crimson triangles in the shape of an hourglass on the underside of its abdomen.

In case you are not aware of it, black widows love to hang out around concrete. I investigated the holes of the fence, and I saw several more spiders.

"Can I get one, Chris?"

"Sure, Mare. It's really easy, even you can do it."

I pulled a straw out of the box and began fishing for a spider. I was so pleased with myself when I caught my first one. We took turns. When we got all the spiders out of the first decoration, we moved down to the next one. After three sections, Chris seemed to be satisfied with twenty spiders, so he screwed the metal lid on the jar. "I think we have enough black widows, Mare. Let's go home."

We walked back slowly to our house in the intense summer heat. When we got home, Chris put the newly captured arachnids in the garage on a shelf. We both went off to find a friend to play with. Mom always told us we could be away from the house if we wanted, but we had to be back by six o'clock to have dinner with the family. It was an important rule in our household.

Several hours later, my dad came home from work. He arrived home like clockwork at 5:15 p.m., Monday through Friday. He and my mom sat at a little bar that separated the kitchen from the dining room and drank highballs, Seagram's, and soda. My mom sat on the kitchen side so she could get up and stir whatever she had cooking on the stove. We ate at six o'clock sharp every evening. My dad was a retired Naval officer and maintained a strict schedule. He needed forty-five minutes to unwind from work, and we were not supposed to bother my parents during this special time.

Dad had just sat down with his drink when I came into the dining room. I knew I wasn't supposed to disturb my parents, but I was excited about my adventure with Chris and so I said, "Hi, Dad."

"Hi, Mimi. How are you?"

"I'm good. Guess what Chris and I did today?"

"What did you and your brother do?"

"We went down to Murrieta and caught a bunch of black widows."

"You did what?"

"We walked down to Murrieta and caught a bunch of black widow spiders."

My dad jumped out of his chair and said, "Where are the spiders, Mimi? Show me where they are."

"They're in a jar in the garage," I said with tears in my eyes. I didn't realize why my dad was so upset. He stormed out to the garage and I followed. I showed him the spiders on the shelf. He grabbed the container and stalked out to the driveway, unscrewed the lid, and dumped all the black widows onto the concrete. My father proceeded to stomp on every single spider, killing them. I stared in horror as he squashed the spiders.

"Mimi don't you ever try to catch black widows again. They are poisonous and if you were to be bitten by one, you could have died!"

By this time, I was crying. I had no idea that they were so dangerous. My dad began to shout for Chris out in front of our house. This was a common form of communication in our neighborhood. Chris rode up on his green stingray bike, looking scared when he saw the fury etched on our father's face.

"What's wrong, Dad?" Chris said nervously.

"You could have killed your little sister or yourself! What were you thinking Christopher Michael Hansen? Go up to your room right now and wait for me there."

I felt sorry for Chris. Even though he probably knew black widows were poisonous, I felt bad about what was going to happen to him. He was going to get the belt. I fled to the backyard to console myself.

Beware of Big Sis

Being the youngest of seven kids had its ups and downs. On the upside, I learned from my siblings, like how to bake a cake, cut out a dress pattern, or catch a toad; better yet, a black widow spider. The downside was I felt left out most of the time. I wanted to do everything that my older siblings were doing. Most of the time they only let me watch, instead of participating. I did, however, learn many lessons from them. Fortunately, I am a visual learner and had a great deal of patience as a five-year-old.

I enjoyed watching my oldest sister, Colleen, prepare a birthday cake; she added the eggs and water to the cake mix before blending it with the hand mixer. She let me pour in the water. My brothers, Mark and Chris, were six and eight years old. They liked to watch her, too, but they had a different agenda from mine; they wanted to lick the cake batter off the silver beaters, rubber spatula, or glass bowl.

Chris was the most impatient. He would keep badgering Colleen, saying, "Hey, Coll, can I lick the beaters yet?"

"No, Chris, I'm not done. I'll let you know, okay?"

So, the three of us watched in anticipation while the process of making a cake went on. Sure enough, Chris would ask again, "Come on,

"Blacky, it's time for you to meet Whitey!" Chris said.

He grabbed the kitten from Jamey's arms, petting it briefly, while Jamey opened the mailbox. Chris gently placed the cat inside, shutting the door tightly, while Jamey pulled up the red flag to make sure the mailman would open it. The mailbox was about twenty inches long, ten inches high, and eight inches wide; the kind you'd see on a country road. The kitten fit inside with room to spare.

"I can't wait to see Whitey's face when he opens the mailbox, huh, Chris?"

"Yeah! Oh boy, this is gonna be great! But Jamey, where're we gonna hide?"

"Good question. Let's look around for bushes or a fence. We need to make sure we can see Whitey and the mailbox from our hiding spot."

"Hey, Jamey, look over at Mrs. Boatright's house See those big juniper bushes? We can hide behind them!"

"Good choice. Let's hope Mrs. Boatright doesn't come out and yell at us."

"Oh, she won't. She sleeps during the day because she works at night."

Chris and Jamey ran over to Mrs. Boatright's house and squatted behind the prickly juniper bushes and waited. It was noon and the bright blue, cloudless sky was beautiful, but it was already getting hot. The summers in Livermore could get up to 110 degrees easily. The sun beat down on their heads while they waited.

"What the heck is taking Whitey so long? My legs are hurting," Jamey complained.

"I know. I'm getting awfully hot and thirsty," Chris said.

"Wait a minute. Shh, here comes Whitey now," Jamey whispered.

The mail car drove slowly in front of Mrs. Railsback's house. The model of her two-story home was the same as Jamey's and ours, but it was a bit fancier because Mr. Railsback was the contractor who helped build the houses in our neighborhood.

Chris and Jamey were bursting with anticipation, their hearts beating wildly in their chests, probably as fast as little Blacky's. They sat still and held their breath as the mail car stopped. Luckily, they had a clear view of the mailbox and Whitey's profile.

Whitey got out of the right-hand side of the vehicle. He was wearing a white pith hat, a baby blue shirt, and gray shorts. He stood on the sidewalk sifting through the stack of letters in his left hand, checking the addresses.

Chris and Jamey squirmed as sweat dripped down their foreheads into their eyebrows. They didn't dare wipe it away because they didn't want to be seen. Their mouths were as dry as a Livermore creek bed in the dead of summer. Their thigh muscles ached from squatting too long. They watched intently while Whitey approached the mailbox, leaning forward to make sure they could see the exchange.

Whitey reached for the knob on the mailbox

and as he opened the door, Blacky's head popped out, mewing loudly. Whitey jumped back in one quick motion and screamed. The letters he had been holding flew in every direction. He looked behind him scanning the area for the culprit who put the cat in the mailbox. He stood for a moment with his hands on his hips, cursing under his breath.

Chris and Jamey slapped their hands over their mouths to keep from laughing out loud. They needed to contain themselves until Whitey was out of earshot.

Meanwhile, Blacky continued to mew from its perch, causing Whitey to turn around. His frown turned into a smile, as he walked over to the mailbox, gently picking up Blacky, he walked to Mrs. Railsback's front porch and tenderly set Blacky down on the cool concrete.

"Now, stay kitty. We both have had enough excitement don't you think? We can't have you getting hurt."

Then Whitey returned to the sidewalk, picked up the mail that was strewn across it, and placed the letters in the mailbox, pushing down the red flag. He hopped into his mail truck and drove to Mrs. Boatright's front yard. Chris and Jamey had kept an eye on Whitey and crept to the opposite side of the junipers staying out of sight.

The boys waited there until Whitey was about five houses down from them before they let out their belly laughs, rolling on the ground.

"Jamey, did you see Whitey's face? Blacky

scared the living daylights out of him!"

"Chris, did you hear Whitey scream like a girl?"

"Sure did. Now, that's what I call a special delivery, Jamey."

Lisa's Backyard

Mary and Lisa

I slammed the door to my house, ran across the street to Lisa's home, and yelled, "Lisa are you ready?" into her bedroom window. It was the first day of summer.

"Almost, Mare. I have a few more chores to do, then we can go. Sorry," she replied.

"That's okay, Lisa. I'll come help. It'll go faster, then we'll have all day to explore."

"Come on in then," she said. Chores, this was a common occurrence with Lisa.

I knocked lightly on her wood-paneled front door and then let myself in. Mrs. Sawyer was in the living room, vacuuming the antique gold sculptured carpet that was already clean. I waved at her, and she looked up at me as she turned off the vacuum.

"Hi, Mary. Lisa has some chores to do before she can play." She smiled.

"I know Mrs. Sawyer. Is it okay if I help her? We want to go exploring today."

"Sure. That's fine." Then Mrs. Sawyer turned the vacuum on again.

Mrs. Sawyer was the only daughter of six children from a German American family who were very strict about cleanliness. My poor friend Lisa had two brothers, but she was the one who did most of the cleaning in the house, just like her mother had done.

I walked back to Lisa's bedroom asking her, "What chore can I do for you today?"

"The breakfast dishes need to be washed, dried, and put away, and the hardwood floors need to be dust mopped," she said apologetically.

"Okay, I'll dust the floors and you do the dishes. We'll get it done quick."

Lisa and I set to our tasks. I grabbed the dust mop out of the hall closet and started with the back hallway and worked my way into the dining room pushing the yellow yarn mop in quick motions across the honey-colored oak floor. By the time I reached the kitchen with a small pile of dust bunnies, Lisa had finished washing the last Franciscan Apple patterned dish. I grabbed a copper dustpan from under the kitchen sink and swept up the dust and crumbs, emptying it into the plastic garbage can in the kitchen. Lisa dried the dishes with a cotton dishtowel embroidered with the word, "Friday" on it.

"All done. Okay, Lisa, let's go. I already made peanut butter and jelly sandwiches for us. I also have some bags of Fritos. We just need some water to drink."

Lisa opened a cabinet and grabbed a silver Thermos and filled it with tap water. Finally, we were ready to go. We headed out her back sliding glass door. The Sawyers hadn't put up a backyard fence, and there was a huge field behind their house that led to the Lincoln Highway less than a mile away.

Lisa and I were mature for our ages, at eight and six years old. I held the brown paper bag with sandwiches, and she carried the thermos. As we walked out into her backyard, the field spread out before us, acres of tall grass and weeds, swaying in the warm summer breeze. I breathed in the fresh scent of the air. I felt a swell of happiness.

This field was my first introduction to nature. My mom was a city girl from New York, so my family didn't go camping like other families. This made me envious because I loved the out-of-doors, the earthy smell of the land, the lovely wildflowers, and all God's creatures.

It was mid-June and school had just let out for the summer, so Lisa and I were eager to explore having been cooped up in a classroom for nine months. The foliage still had some greenness to it and a sweet fragrance wafted up to our noses as we traipsed through the broken plant shafts. There was a variety of colors in the field: lavender, white, coral, and pink flowers;

green and gold grass, all looked stunning against the cerulean sky.

Lisa and I could hear the melodious call of the meadowlarks, but we couldn't see them. We listened to the wheezing song of the redwing blackbirds, with their jet black feathers and bright scarlet underwings. Their talons clasped the tall weeds, swinging back and forth. Hundreds of vibrant orange California poppies spread out before us in a clearing. I picked one because of its beauty. Lisa, being older, quickly reprimanded me saying, "Mary, don't pick another poppy. They are the state flower and it's against the law to pick them. A policeman will come and take you to jail!"

I stared at her in horror and said, "Really? I didn't know, Lisa."

"Here, Mare. Let's bury the flower and no one will ever know." So we dug a little hole and covered up the evidence. We walked on looking for any creature we could find. We spooked a jackrabbit, and he took off running at full speed across the field, his huge powerful brown legs kicking out behind him. He had extremely long black-tipped ears, sticking up tall and thin, as he galloped away looking for a better hiding place.

We continued walking and, in the distance, we spotted an old wooden barn. Its roof sagged in the middle like an old broken-down nag. The huge barn door was ajar. We wanted to go in, but we were too scared of trespassing on someone's property. We knew that some of the

between my toes. I discovered I could leave footprints as I walked in the soft wet sand. I couldn't wait to look for shells. I began to scan the sand and rugged rocks, and I found many limpet, muscle, and turban shells. As we walked along the dunes, Chris noticed a piece of shell poking out of the hill, and as we began to dig, we found ten abalone shells buried in the sand. Several were intact, the size of dinner plates, with swirling colors of pink, green, and blue, inside the shell. Several of the shells were broken by age and erosion.

We stashed the shells and continued to scramble over the jagged rocks and look for more creatures in the tide pools. We saw many green sea anemones, purple sea urchins, and bright orange crabs. The rocks were very sharp, and I scraped my hands and knees. Far off in the distance, I could see seals sunbathing on the rocks and making barking noises.

Going back up the hill to the motel was much more difficult. My leg muscles strained to turn the bike pedals to get up the steep hill. As we reached the top, we were amazed to see four deer crossing the road in front of us. I had never seen a live deer, and I was very excited. We stopped our bikes and watched them silently with awe. They daintily walked across the street on long, thin legs. We looked into their big brown eyes as they took one last look at us before disappearing behind the Cypress trees.

We slowly rode the rest of the way back to the motel, parked our bikes, and entered the room. We tossed our bounty on Chris's bed. We gazed at all the beautiful shells we collected. Then to our amazement, some of them began to crawl across the bedspread. We did not realize that some of our treasures were hermit crabs.

Later that evening, after dinner, we all piled into the station wagon and Dad drove us down to the beach. All we had was the moon and stars to light our way. I felt the ocean breeze caress my skin and heard the waves crash in the distance. As we got closer to the surf, I saw to my amazement tiny lights shining in the water. I whispered to my parents, "Are there stars in the water?"

"Mimi," said my father, "Those are called phosphorescence. They are tiny creatures that give off their own light."

I had never seen anything like it in my seven short years of life. It was a truly magical experience. I will never forget what wonderful memories were made during my first trip of many to Pacific Grove.

The Summer of '69

I t was the summer of 1969; the year man first stepped on the moon. It also happened to be one of the hottest summers on record in Livermore, California. I remember day after day, temperatures over 100 degrees during July. Since our family home didn't have air conditioning, the only way to beat the heat was to go swimming at the local pool, May Nissen.

One hot July day, my mom handed me fifty cents, and I flew out the door like a prisoner escaping from her cell. I raced across the street to my friend Lisa's house to rescue her. She was nine and I was seven years old that summer. I was wearing my turquoise one-piece bathing suit. I had a shabby white towel rolled up with my pink bathing cap inside under my right arm and two quarters gripped tightly in my left hand. Lisa wore a faded yellow bathing suit with her towel rolled under her arm. We were both barefoot and walked three-quarters of a mile to the pool, relieved to be out of our houses for the next four hours.

On this day, we left early because we knew there would be a long line. The pool was open from one to four, Monday through Friday. It was 117 degrees in Livermore that day, a record high. When we arrived, about fifty kids and moms snaked in a line coming out of the building. It was so hot, we were sweating, our faces red as tomatoes. Finally, the line began to move at a snail's pace. We entered the pool building entrance and felt the coolness of the cinder block walls and handed our twenty-five cents to the pool attendant. Lisa and I went into the locker room, put on our caps, took our showers, and raced out to the pool.

For the next three hours we jumped, splashed, and played tea party under the water. We really couldn't swim, with a hundred other excited children in the pool. At 3:55 p.m., the lifeguards blew their shiny silver whistles to tell us it was time to leave the pool. Lisa and I got out reluctantly, our eyes stinging from the chlorine. We immediately pulled off our constricting bathing caps because they gave us headaches and left wavy lines across our foreheads. We skipped to the snack shack and bought Sweet Tart necklaces, which cost ten cents each. We put them around our necks, chewing a few candies off at a time. The necklaces left colorful rainbow rings around our necks from the dampness of our hair.

We headed to the Dairy Queen, which was right next door to the pool. We each got a chocolate-dipped ice cream cone with our remaining fifteen cents. After we got our cones, we sat inside on the aqua colored stools and twirled around. The store had air conditioning, and we took our time eating so we could enjoy the coolness of the store. First, we broke off the hardened chocolate, piece by piece, trying to make it last, each of us waiting to see who could take the longest time before taking a bite of the ice cream. Then we slowly licked our ice cream, and when that was finished, we crunched down our cones. When we finished our treat, we walked home in the intense white heat. Our towels were wet, and we put them over our shoulders to keep us cool and protect us from the sun.

We arrived home, happy and tired from our day. Our eyes were bloodshot and blurry from the chlorine, but we still had our candy necklaces to enjoy until dinnertime.

Those summer days were a wonderful time in my innocent young life. They helped me forget about the chaos that was going on in the world in 1969. I appreciated the companionship of my best friend, Lisa, and the fun of splashing in the water and the sweet taste of candy and ice cream. All that happiness for a mere fifty cents.

The Mysterious Christmas Gift

I was eight years old the Christmas of 1970. Three years before, Chris boastfully told me Santa did not exist. I was devastated. Once my parents found out I did not believe in Santa, they began to put the gifts under the tree before Christmas Day.

When December hit, I felt giddy. I always looking forward to decorating the tree and watching the gifts slowly pile up under it. I loved to look at the shape and size of each gift and imagine what was inside the shiny wrapping paper.

Chris, on the other hand, was a cheater. When our mom and dad were asleep in their bedroom, he sneaked under the tree and carefully remove the tape to peek inside his presents. I caught him once and said, "Chris, what's the fun of seeing what your gifts are? Wouldn't you rather be surprised?"

"No, Mare, I like to know what I'm getting," he retorted.

When Christmas morning finally arrived, I was amazed at the number of presents stacked under the tree. It was mainly since I had six siblings. I opened my gifts one by one, savoring each moment. I received mostly clothes from my parents. A mini dress in navy blue polyester with long red sleeves and a red heart on the front. I also got two pairs of stretch pants in green and lavender with striped tops to match.

I opened the next gift, which was a doll. My mom loved dolls and bought me one every other year. This year, she picked out a black doll with curly ebony hair. She was unique because her arms, legs, and tummy were inflated with air, and when I squeezed each one, it made a sound in a different key on the musical scale. I could play songs with this doll. I loved her. My mom knew I enjoyed music and singing, so it was the perfect gift for me.

The last present I opened was in a big box. It was from Chris and Mark. I tore off the wrapping paper and inside was a slightly smaller box, and when I unwrapped that one, there was a smaller box inside of that. You get the picture. Inside the fifth box was a small piece of paper with writing on it. I read the words out loud. *Mary, to get your gift, you need to find the clues around the house. Go to the kitchen pantry. Look for the snowman cookie tin and look inside.*

I giggled with excitement. This was going to be a fun treasure hunt! My parents and siblings watched as I ran to the pantry and opened the folding doors. On the middle shelf was the tin. I opened it up and pulled the paper out and read, *Go to the linen closet upstairs and find your next clue in a small box.* I ran upstairs, flung open the wooden doors, and found the small white box. I lifted the lid and pulled out the next clue. *Go to the hearth. The next clue is under the Leprechaun statue.* I ran downstairs to the living room where everyone watched me with anticipation as I picked up the leprechaun that sat next to the fireplace. I grabbed the small slip of paper and read the clue out loud for all to hear. *Mary, go look under your bed, and there you will find your gift.*

I ran upstairs quickly with Mark and Chris at my heels. I bolted into my room, knelt on the rug, and pulled up my orange bedspread, my heart beating wildly. When I saw my gift I laughed with delight. My brothers had given me the game of Clue.

Mrs. Tarin

Mrs. Tarin was my fourth grade teacher and I loved her dearly. I looked up to her in every way. She seldom yelled at her students, but if she did, they deserved it. She was the kind of teacher that I wanted to have in every grade in school, but sadly I knew it was not possible.

Mrs. Tarin was very pretty. She had long, wavy chestnut hair and bright blue eyes. She had classic facial features that made me look at her twice. I think she was about thirty-five years old when I was her student in 1971. She always wore fashionable dresses in bright colors.

Mrs. Tarin was a gifted teacher. I could tell she loved us students, and she had the patience of a saint. She always made me feel good about myself with her words of encouragement. Even when my penmanship was atrocious, she would gently say, "Try again, Mary." Because I was left-handed, it was always a challenge for teachers to show me how to form my letters correctly, especially in cursive.

Fourth grade was my favorite grade in school because I got to learn my favorite subjects: California history, Native Americans, and California Missions. The mission I studied was San Juan Capistrano. I remember making my mission out of sticky dough and Popsicle sticks. I used my creativity by making a headdress of multicolored feathers and a bead bracelet. I was in heaven.

My favorite part of the school day was storytime after lunch. We all sat quietly at our desks with our heads laid down on our hands and listened to Mrs. Tarin read a book. I loved the way her soft voice crescendoed with emotion when a character in the story got angry. My two favorite books she read were *James and the Giant Peach* and *Charlie and the Chocolate Factory*.

Mrs. Tarin made all the characters come alive by the inflection of her voice, and each day I looked forward to the next chapter. I read all of Roald Dahl's books to my children while they were growing up, and I think they enjoyed the stories just as much as I did as a child.

I believe Mrs. Tarin was the reason I became a teacher. She instilled in me the love of learning that has stayed with me my entire life. I became a teacher when my youngest child, Sam, was in the first grade. I enjoyed being a stay-at-home mom and wanted to care for my children and not have someone else raise them. I studied human development in college.

When Sam entered first grade, he struggled with reading and writing. Several other boys in his class were disciplinary challenges to the teacher, and Sam was overlooked. The elementary school threatened to close, so I searched for an alternative school for Sam.

I heard about an open house at Valley Montessori School in town. I made an appointment to observe a classroom. While I observed the children and teacher in the class, I knew immediately that was where Sam needed to go to school, and I wanted to teach. I was very impressed with the Montessori philosophy: follow the child. That means to help each child and meet his or her needs by teaching them at their developmental level. I began to substitute teach and then took a Montessori training certificate class during the summer. By August, I began my student teaching year. I taught ages three to six.

It was no surprise my favorite part of teaching was to read stories to my students, as well as teaching them to read. It was always exciting to hear a child read his or her first word or finish reading their first book. The elation expressed on their young faces was fantastic to witness. I also loved music, and I played my guitar and sang every day with my students. The children responded positively to music. We had a pet parakeet named Pinky in the classroom. Every time we sang a song, Pinky tweeted along with us, and we loved it.

So, Mrs. Tarin, wherever you are, thank you so much for my wonderful and magical fourth grade school year. It is a gift I will never forget.

Colleen's Wedding Day

Colleen and Conley

T he sky was clear, and the sun shone down on a crisp fall morning. It was October 8, 1972, Colleen's wedding day. Our house was full of excited family members who couldn't wait for the upcoming nuptials. I was ten years old and bursting with anticipation to see my sister get married. Peggy had married in New Mexico the year before, and I never got over not being invited to her ceremony, so this wedding was a very big deal to me.

I always dreamed of being a flower girl, but my window of opportunity closed on that position. All the flower girls I had seen were between the ages of three and seven, and I was too mature to be suited for the task. My mom, however, seemed to know how much I wanted to have a special dress and took me to the most expensive children's clothing store in Livermore, which was ironically named Hansen's Children's Wear, (my maiden name was Hansen). I picked out the most beautiful blush pink sateen dress with a pink rosebud and satin bow that tied at my waist. It was lovely and cost an exorbitant $40. I couldn't believe my mom paid the price, but I was so happy she did. I felt beautiful when I wore that dress.

My mom chose for herself a lemon yellow Jackie Kennedy style dress with a matching jacket, and she looked gorgeous. She was forty-five years old at the time and was a very attractive brunette with striking light blue eyes and a slender figure. She had her hair done for the special occasion. It was her firstborn's wedding day, and she wanted to look her best.

I remember my three brothers, Pat, Chris, and Mark, trying to find adequate clothing for the occasion. I think my mom kind of dropped the ball on that one because my brothers were wearing their Easter clothes that were too small for them, the pants short by an inch or two.

Katy looked amazing in a long maxi dress made of burgundy jersey print that clung to her curvaceous figure. Her long blonde hair was brushed to perfection. Peggy's long dark brown hair looked lovely, and her dress of autumn colors and long, velvet brown vest was stylish.

That left my father, who was still getting ready. I had never seen him in a tuxedo, and when he came out of his room, he looked very handsome. He was swearing because a piece of his outfit was missing—the ruffles to his shirt. For those of us who lived during the seventies, it was all about the tux with a ruffled shirt and bow tie; it was as common as sliced bread.

Colleen's called her fiancé, Conley, to tell him that he had to go to Southland Mall to pick up my dad's ruffles, and he said he would. He lived in Hayward and it wouldn't be too much trouble.

Colleen was the last to come out of her room, and when she did, I was in awe of how beautiful she looked in her white wedding gown and veil and her beaming face. We were all set to go to St. Charles Church and the wedding was to begin at two o'clock. We arrived at 1:15 p.m. and Colleen went into the chapel to be hidden from sight.

The guests started to arrive at 1:45 p.m. and the excitement began to build. The wedding was being held in the chapel because Conley wasn't Catholic. The priest at St. Michael's would not marry my sister and Conley, so Father Dollard agreed to marry them at St. Charles, in the chapel, which seemed like a good compromise.

The guests were all seated by two o'clock, and Dad was pacing, complaining that he didn't have his ruffles. Fifteen minutes later, he was more agitated and inebriated. By 2:55 p.m., Colleen was beside herself because Conley had not yet arrived. This was before cell phones, and we had no idea why Conley was late.

Finally, at three o'clock, Conley arrived with his best man, Michael Smith, his cousin. They handed the ruffles to my dad and he quickly put them on, grabbed Colleen, and walked her down the aisle. By then, my dad was three sheets to the wind. Their friend, Bill Wilcox was playing "Greensleeves" on his guitar, and the ceremony went beautifully. There was a sense of relief from everyone in the chapel that the wedding had gone on without a hitch—well almost.

We all headed to the Elks Lodge in Springtown for the reception. After the delay of the wedding, everyone was ready for food, drink, and fun. My family members and friends did not hesitate to start eating food from the buffet and drinking champagne.

When the band began to play, the Hansen clan really shined, dancing up a storm on the dance floor. I will never forget seeing my dad dancing the Polka with my Aunt Betty for the first time in my life. I was amazed that he was a great dancer.

I had been so preoccupied with having fun that finally I noticed that the people who sat in the other half of the hall were quietly watching the Hansens and their friends having a blast. I realized that my new brother-in-law's family was not partaking in the merriment because they were Southern Baptist and didn't drink alcohol or dance. It was something I had never experienced before and foreign to me. I thought, How sad, they are missing all the fun. It's so ironic because Conley's last name is O'Neal and is of Irish ancestry. I wondered when they stopped being Catholic and become Baptist?

Colleen's wedding day was probably the most fun I had ever had up to that point. Everyone in my family was happy and having a great time, and I felt somewhat grown-up being a part of the celebration. Colleen and Conley are still married and will celebrate their forty-eighth wedding anniversary this coming October. I am so glad that I have such fond memories of that special day.

Eating Issues

D innertime was a very important daily ritual in my large family. Being the youngest of seven children most definitely molded me into the person I am today, especially my eating habits.

Some of my first memories are at the dinner table with my mom and dad and three brothers and three sisters. We had a picnic table in our kitchen, which we used because it was big enough to fit our family. We didn't have much money to spend on furniture, so it was our best option. It had a red and white checked oilcloth on top, just like the *Waltons* on TV. My family sat at the table while I sat in my highchair.

You would think it would be noisy at mealtimes, but it was not because my dad was a retired Naval officer, and there was never much talking at dinner; my dad wouldn't tolerate it. If the conversation got too rambunctious, all my dad had to do was look into the eyes of the perpetrator making the noise and stare them down.

We always said our Catholic prayer together before eating. "Bless us our Lord for these thy gifts, which we are about to receive from thy bounty, through Christ our Lord, Amen." A few times I started singing at the table, and my dad said, "Mimi, no singing at the table."

Chris always sat to my dad's right because

Chris was always up to mischief. My dad wanted him within arm's reach so he could give him a smack if needed. Chris was usually bothering Mark or me by pinching or kicking us under the table. We each had our favorite drinking glass, and Chris licked his to make sure we didn't take it from him.

When I was very little and I sat in the highchair, my mom always made sure I had enough food. But when I turned four and sat in a regular chair, it was every child for themselves. On Sundays, my mom always cooked baked chicken. She cut up two chickens and baked the pieces with crushed Cornflakes and milk to a golden brown and then served it on a big platter. As soon as that plate touched the middle of the table, the pieces of steaming hot chicken magically disappeared before my eyes, snatched up by my stronger, older siblings. I learned very quickly that if I didn't grab a drumstick fast enough, I would have to settle for a scrawny wing. But I had to be careful if I took too much food because I had to eat everything on my plate before I could be excused. My mother used to say, "Mimi, it is a sin to waste food. Did you know that there are children starving in Africa?"

If I remember correctly, I always ate all my food except for when my mom put peas on my plate. I hated peas. I sat for a long time looking at them with tears in my eyes, turning to my dad, hoping for mercy. My mom would say, "Mimi, you may be excused when you have eaten all your peas." Finally, I slowly scooped them up with my fork tried to swallow them, gagging the entire time. Once I had choked them down, I could be excused and take my plate to the sink.

There also began to be another incentive to clear my plate. A few times a week, my mom bought dessert at the grocery store, and the only way to attain some was by eating everything on my dish. My mom was not a baker, so she bought a frozen Sara Lee cheesecake with strawberries on top (one of my favorites), frozen eclairs, frozen Pepperidge Farm layered cake, or Neapolitan ice cream. I thought these desserts were delicious until I ate homemade desserts at other people's homes as I got older.

I had to eat all my food before I could eat a sugary dessert. This, unfortunately, led me into a life of being on the slightly pudgy side. It is still very difficult for me to leave food on my plate without feeling guilty.

Another terrible eating habit I acquired was eating too quickly. This was caused by the fact that I couldn't get a second helping of food unless I ate the first. Leftovers were rare in our house. So, if I ate too slowly and was still hungry, I was out of luck. This started a habit of eating my food too fast.

My oldest brother Pat was the fastest eater in our house. My siblings used to call him the human vacuum. Pat was not a big talker, so dinnertime was all about food and the consumption of it. He dished up his food, and a minute later it was gone. My mom used to yell at him saying, "Patrick, quit inhaling your food."

My mother cooked a variety of foods, but mostly it was meat and potatoes because that's what my dad liked. Some of my favorite dinners were chicken and dumplings, corned beef and cabbage, meatloaf and mashed potatoes, pot roast, and spaghetti and meatballs, which she only made for special occasions.

My least favorite dish that she cooked was kidney stew, which was a traditional Irish meal. I not only hated it, I detested it. I couldn't even be in the house when the kidneys were cooking because of the stinky smell of urea in the air. Luckily, my mother only cooked this stew about once or twice a year. My mom started talking about making it a few days before she bought the kidneys, so I had a heads up. Then I planned which friend I wanted to have dinner with in the neighborhood.

My most sympathetic ally was Mrs. Boatright. She was a single, divorced mother of five, who worked nights in the ER at Alta Bates, in Berkeley. On some mornings, I went to the Boatright's and told Sherry we were having kidney stew. She talked to her mom later in the day, and I would be invited to dinner. When I informed my mom, she just laughed. I tolerated my mom's liver and onions, but the kidney stew was out of the question.

I learned how to cook from my mom, and I am grateful to her. I also appreciated all the meals she prepared for my family. I am happy that when I was in high school, my dad began to take my mom out to dinner on Friday nights to give her a break. She deserved to be taken out to dinner after all those years of cooking. Also, they could finally afford to go out with only a few kids left at home. I can't even imagine how much it costs to feed a family of nine today.

Cecilia and Sam

Cecilia and Sam

Growing up in a big family made it difficult to convince my mom to get a pet. We children begged and pleaded, but to no avail. My mom would not budge. She told us seven children that she had enough to take care of around the house and that was that.

When I was six years old, Colleen brought home a rabbit for an Easter present for us three youngest kids. Mark, Chris, and I were thrilled. I don't think Colleen asked permission from our parents; she just brought the rabbit home and when my mom saw it, she couldn't resist because the rabbit was so cute. He had a white body with gray ears, nose, and tail and his eyes were pink. We decided to name him Sam, after my dad's father, whom we never met. We didn't have a cage for Sam, so we just let him run around in the backyard eating grass. He made a den in a pampas grass bush in our yard. It made a great home because the blades would cut us if we tried to grab Sam out of his well-protected home.

Sam was fun to look at, but he never became tame. I couldn't catch him to cuddle with, so he wasn't like a real pet. But my parents were fine with having Sam because they didn't have to care for him and he was cheap; he just ate grass and carrots.

I still wanted a pet of my own, and a few years later, my dad brought home a chicken as an Easter present for me. I couldn't believe it. My own pet. The chicken was small and had black and white feathers. She was a Bantam chicken, about ten inches tall, and never would be large like a Rhode Island Red that grows to about 20 inches tall. I was so excited to name my pet. What a big responsibility. I wanted it to fit her personality. I thought and thought. I ran through all the names in my mind that I had come across in my nine years and decided on Cecilia. It was my mom's middle name, and I thought it fit my chicken perfectly. She looked like a Cecilia.

I wanted Cecilia to be safe from the cats in our neighborhood, so I built her a coop out of scraps of plywood we had in our garage. It was about two feet wide by three feet long and eighteen inches high with one end open. I rounded her up at night and put the box against the sliding glass door so she couldn't get out. It was also fun because I could look at her from inside the house through the glass door.

When I woke up in the morning, I ran outside and pulled the box away from the glass door and talked to Cecilia. She followed me wherever I went in the backyard. If I ran, she ran after me. It was so funny. I didn't know about how animals can imprint on a human back when I was little, but she thought I was her mama.

A few months went by and one morning when I went down to look at Cecilia in her coop, there was a perfectly formed nest made of straw, and in the middle was a beautiful little brown egg. I couldn't believe it. She had never made a nest before. How could she do that? I ran into the house yelling for my brothers, sisters, and parents to come see Cecilia's beautiful egg. Everyone was so surprised when they saw it.

From that day on, Cecilia laid an egg every other day. It was so much fun to take her egg out of the coop and put it in the refrigerator. No one seemed to want to eat her eggs. I don't know if it was because they were brown or because she was a pet. I think my mom cooked the eggs when we weren't looking because they eventually got used up.

As Cecilia got older, her feathers grew and she could fly up into the high bushes in our yard, but she never flew out of our backyard. I guess she knew where her home was and didn't want to leave. She and Sam the rabbit became friends. Until one day when a big marmalade colored cat came into our yard. I could always tell when a cat came into our yard because Cecilia clucked loud when she got scared. That cat crouched down and stalked Cecilia. Before I could get out the door, the cat started chasing Cecilia. Sam ran up to that big cat, whipped his back legs around, and kicked the cat in the face with his big strong hind legs. I was in shock and couldn't believe what I had witnessed.

Sam saved Cecilia's life. Sam was a hero and protected his friend Cecilia. I told my family what happened, but they didn't believe me. This same scenario happened again and again with that cat, Cecilia, and Sam, and I was finally vindicated when my brother, Mark, saw it too.

I had Cecilia about three years, and then my parents made me get rid of her. Dad and Mom said the chicken poop was stinking up the backyard. I was twelve years old and very sad and wanted to find her a good home. I found out that Lisa had a friend who lived on the outskirts of town on a ranch that had chickens. She told Lisa she would take Cecilia.

Lisa made the arrangements for her mom to drive us out to the ranch. I was crying when I put Cecilia into the big chicken coop. It had eight Rhode Island Red chickens that towered over my little Cecilia. I was afraid for her. They were already pecking at her. I couldn't watch anymore; I had to leave. I don't know whatever happened to Cecilia, and I don't want to know because I don't think she came to a good end. I just try to think about the fun we had together when I was growing up and the miraculous relationship between her and Sam. I wonder if Sam ever missed Cecilia's company.

The Tomboy

S teve was my nemesis when I was a kid. Mark and he were in the same grade at Rincon Elementary School. I was one grade younger. Steve lived on Pine Street, three blocks from our house on Sunset Drive. Steve had a kid brother named Scotty who was two years younger than me, and I didn't care much for him either. He was almost as bad as his older brother as far as picking on me, but I was a head taller than Scotty and that gave me some clout. I didn't see the brothers much during the school year, but during the summertime, I ran into them quite often.

I loved school. Social Studies was my favorite subject, but when school let out for the summer, I was ecstatic. The first couple of weeks of summer, I played with the girls in my neighborhood, but then the girl drama got too intense, so I fell back to who I was first and foremost: a tomboy. Because I had three older brothers who were closer to my age than my three sisters, it was natural that I would want to follow them around and do activities that they did. Pat was my oldest brother, eight years older, so I didn't hang out with him much. Pat preferred working with his model trains or looking at his coin and stamp collections, which were all inside hobbies.

I liked to be outside, away from the sickening

cigarette smoke that was produced by my chain-smoking mom and dad. I had been a sickly child, getting bronchitis several times a year, not knowing back then my parents' secondhand smoke was the cause. The older I got, the healthier I became because I was out of the house more often. By the time I was seven years old, I left the house at nine o'clock and didn't return until six o'clock for dinner during the summer. I might pop in the house quickly to go to the bathroom, get a snack, or change into my swimsuit, but that was about it.

When my girlfriends got too "girly," I switched it up and hung out with Mark, Chris, and the other boys from my neighborhood. Being around boys was less complicated. We got on our bikes with bats, baseballs, and gloves in hand, and rode to Rincon School's baseball diamond three blocks away. Mark kept the stats, and Chris usually picked the teams. There was an unwritten rule that brothers shouldn't be on the same team, and boy, were there a lot of brothers: Giovanni and Ray, Joe and Bruce, Steve and Scotty, Greg and Tooter, and my brothers, Chris and Mark. Then there were some kids like Brian and Jamey whose brothers were older and didn't play with us. And then there was me, who didn't fit into any of these categories.

My brothers taught me how to play baseball and I held my own. Most of the boys lived on our street or around the corner on Norfolk Road. They were used to having me around, but Steve and Scotty didn't want me playing with them. They always harassed me and said to my brothers, "Does *she* have to play? We don't want her on *our* team!"

I have to say, I loved that my brothers stuck up for me. Of course, at home, Chris teased me most of the time, but if anyone else messed with his little sister, they had to answer to him. Chris was the strongest and most feared boy in our neighborhood.

I put up with Steve and Scotty for several years. It got to the point that I pretty much ignored their taunting. Until one day, when I was eleven, I snapped.

The night was warm and sultry. The sun had just set, and I could see Venus winking brightly in the dusky sky. All the kids from our neighborhood were out playing in the street. Some were riding bikes, others were roller skating. I was in front of Mrs. Boatright's house. She had five kids and her daughter Sherry was my age. We were on her front lawn doing cartwheels, walkovers, and handsprings. Doing gymnastics was one of my favorite activities at the time; I pretended to be Olga Korbut who had just won three Gold medals in the Summer Olympics that year.

Steve had ridden his bike over to my street to hang out with my brothers, but first, he rode over near me and began harassing me, saying, "Mary, you are *not* Olga Korbut, that's for sure. You can't even do a decent handstand."

I don't know what possessed me that

evening, but I had put up with Steve for the last three years, and I couldn't take his taunting anymore. I ran over to him while he was sitting on his chartreuse Stingray bike and started socking him. Steve did not see that coming and yelled, "Mary, what the heck are you doing?" He had fallen off his bike at this point, his forearms up in front of his face fending me off.

I was screaming at him, "I am sick and tired of you. Leave me alone, Steve." Finally, I stopped hitting him and he hopped on his bike and quickly rode away. I felt shaky, but then a warm glow washed over me, and I started laughing. Sherry had witnessed the entire scene and said, "Mary, you just beat up Steve. I can't believe it."

Steve never bothered me again. I see him from time to time at funerals and parties, and he gives me a hug. He is a handsome man, over six feet tall. I wonder if he ever thinks of the time I beat him up all those years ago. I think about it every time I see him and smile.

Karen

When I was eleven years old and in sixth grade, a new girl named Karen came into my class. She was a quiet girl with a pinched white face, long dark brown hair, and very thin. Her clothes were rumpled and old like they had just been purchased from the Salvation Army and were not washed and ironed.

I made it a point to speak to Karen to get to know her. She became my friend. She lived over in the older part of town with her mother, a single parent, in a tiny two-bedroom, one-bathroom home. I rode to her house after school with my twenty-five cents, and we bought a McDonald's soda in a reusable cup with pictures of Ronald McDonald and friends. It was convenient because she lived very close to the fast-food restaurant.

For several weeks, Karen was made fun of by some of the kids in our class, but especially by a girl named Lena. She was the bully girl at Rincon Elementary School. She also made fun of the special needs kids or anyone who was different in some way. Karen became her target, and Lena ridiculed Karen any chance she got.

One day, it became unbearable to me. I felt so bad for Karen. I knew her clothes and where she lived embarrassed her, but it wasn't her fault. Lena was especially brutal that day. Karen and I went out to the playground at recess and sat on a bench. Lena came over to us. She made fun of Karen and stuck her face between us as we sat on the bench. Something in me snapped. I said, "Lena don't you ever say mean words to Karen again," and then I slapped Lena across the face. I think we were all shocked. Lena stepped back and her friend Macy said, "Lena, hit her back. Don't let Mary get away with that." But Lena didn't hit me. She didn't bother Karen or me again.

I have never forgotten that moment. Although I don't condone violence, there are just times when it is the only thing that will stop a bully. As the years went by, Lena told other kids how she could beat me up if she wanted to, but she never touched me. I knew she was secretly afraid of me.

I showed courage that day. I stood up to that bully. The last time I saw Lena, she was nineteen, unwed, and pregnant. I felt sorry for her. I don't know what happened to Karen because she moved away a few years later. But I will always feel a sense of pride that I stood up for her when she was unable to stand up for herself.

Going to the Movies with Mom and Dad

I have a very distinct memory of going to the movies with my mom and dad in 1973. I remember it so clearly because there were very few times I went to the movies with Dad. I am not sure what possessed him to go. Maybe it was the movie that enticed him: *American Graffiti*. Maybe the film brought back fond memories of the 1950s when he and my mom were young had fewer children and less responsibility. Anyway, it was a memorable experience for me.

It was a regular Saturday afternoon in our household when dad announced that he was taking us to see a movie that evening. I think he wanted to see the newly renovated Vine Theater, which was the only one in town. Instead of a huge screen, they split the theater into two parts so two movies could be shown at the same time. The Vine originally opened on December 26, 1956, and I am sure that it made quite a sensation in the sleepy cowtown of Livermore. I wish I could have been there to share in the festivities.

Raring to go, Mark and I hopped into Dad's metallic-green 1972 Oldsmobile that still had that new car smell. We waited impatiently for Dad to drive us to the theater. I wasn't sure why my other brothers and sisters were not coming with us, but I realized later, that older kids didn't go to the movies with their parents, and I found out why.

As we entered the Vine, the wonderful smell of fresh popcorn and butter enveloped us, and my stomach rumbled in response. The well-lit candy counter beckoned us to come closer to look at what was offered in their brilliant multicolored boxes. Dad bought us popcorn, sodas, and Junior Mints, those dark chocolate disks filled with wintergreen. What a fabulous combination.

We walked carefully down the dimly lit aisle carrying our food and drink to select our seats. Mom and Dad sat down first. Mark promptly took a seat directly in front of them, and I followed his lead. We were getting to that age where being with your parents was a little embarrassing. I was twelve and he was thirteen.

I was excited to see a movie because I didn't get to go to the movies very often. I had no idea what the movie was about, but that didn't matter. I was ready to be entertained. For those of you who haven't seen *American Graffiti*, it did entertain the viewer. It had many funny scenes, serious scenes, but unfortunately, it had some sexy scenes, which mortified me. I couldn't believe I was watching the movie with my parents right behind me. Ugh.

Overall, I am glad that I went to see that movie with my parents. It was a classic of sorts and brings back a sense of nostalgia when I watch it now. The town of Livermore was much like the town in the movie. I heard that it was filmed in Modesto, California. I am fortunate that I got to share that unforgettable evening with Mom and Dad.

Middle School Memories

Mary at thirteen

Back when Barbra Streisand's song, "The Way We Were" was the #1 hit on the music charts, the movie, *Blazing Saddles* premiered, President Nixon resigned, and I entered seventh grade at Junction Avenue Middle School in Livermore, California. It was a time of change and turmoil in America.

I had my own anxiety. I was nervous about starting school on September third. That was back when school started after Labor Day like it should. I ruminated for a week about what I was going to wear on my first day. I ended up choosing burgundy corduroy pants, a white long-sleeved turtleneck bodysuit, and a pink and burgundy argyle sweater vest because fashions were becoming more conservative at that time in contrast to the skimpy outfits of the hippy generation.

My wavy, reddish-brown hair cascaded down the middle of my back, and I had an innocent baby face. I was five feet tall and weighed 100 pounds. I remember that clearly because I had a Naval Medical ID card made for me at Oak Knoll Hospital. A corpsman had weighed me and measured my height, which was so embarrassing.

Attending Junction was a whole different ball game compared to Rincon Elementary School I previously attended. Girls were mean and cliquey in middle school. I didn't know who I was going to hang out with. The first day, I ended up going solo the mile and a half to Junction on my royal blue Schwinn bike. I had gotten my list of classes in the mail the previous week. It listed English, Social Studies, Math, P.E., Band, Art, and Science.

Social Studies had always been my favorite subject, and I hoped for a nice teacher. When I met Mrs. Becker, I instantly bonded with her. She was in her early 60s, with short, salt and pepper hair and bright pink lipstick. She wore blue plastic-framed glasses, a turquoise squash blossom necklace, long denim skirt, and moccasins. She was a bit eccentric, but that's what made her so interesting. Mrs. Becker's dry sense of humor and quirkiness made the class entertaining, which was good since it followed lunch.

I knew a few girls from Rincon in a couple of my classes, and we started to hang out. They weren't the best girls to be around because they had started smoking cigarettes in the field during lunchtime and were trying to act tough toward other students. I didn't want to smoke. I had lived with inhaling secondhand smoke from my parent's cigarettes for the last twelve years. After a few months, I had had enough of these girls' bad habits and split from them. They didn't take it well.

Three months after school started, Lena, the leader of the group, came up to me in her tight bell-bottom jeans and halter top. She had her "hench girl," Macy with her, who was five foot ten. I was at my locker when they cornered me, and Lena yelled, "Mary, what the hell is going on? Why don't you hang around us anymore? Do you think you are too good for us? You have always been a goody-two-shoes."

I stood there staring at her in astonishment until I gathered my courage and said, "Lena, we don't like the same things. I am not better than you. I am different from you. I have other interests."

Lena stammered, "Yeah, sure, Mary. We don't need you anyhow." She and Macy left me, and I watched them stomp down the concrete walkway. I felt such joy. I had wanted to break away from them for a long time, and I finally did it. I could start fresh and try to find new friends, ones with similar values and interests like mine. I knew it wouldn't be easy, but anything was possible.

I enjoyed learning in school, and I focused on my studies. I made the principal's honor roll each semester during my two years at Junction. My school had always been given a bad reputation. The other kids in town called our school, "Junkyard." So, we retaliated telling the kids from Mendenhall that they went to "Mental-hall." Years later, three of my children, Alana, Amando, and Colton attended Junction. They all received the Presidential Academic Award at graduation.

I learned so much from Mrs. Becker. Her class made me smile. She taught us interesting facts about ancient civilizations: the Greeks, Romans, and Egyptians. We made Roman Arches out of clay, make clay tablets with cuneiform symbols with a wooden stick, and learned to write the Greek alphabet.

I continued to enjoy Mrs. Becker's class until the last few weeks of school when she announced to the class, "Everyone, for your final project, you each will have to give an oral presentation to the class. You get to choose your own subject. It can be anything that has to do with history in this country or the world. It needs to be five minutes long, and you must bring materials to enhance your written report."

"Oh gosh. I can't get up in front of the class and talk. I've never done that before," I said to Jennifer, a girl who sat across from me. She looked at me sympathetically. I decided to do my report on the history of the American flag. I had an old flag that had been my grandfather William Claffy's. It was given to his wife, my grandmother, when he died. He had been in WWI and was given a military funeral. The flag had forty-eight stars on it. Grandpa Claffy died in 1957 before Alaska and Hawaii became states.

I wrote a detailed report on the history of our country's flag. I practiced reading it in front of the mirror in our upstairs bathroom at home. I thought I was ready, but when that fateful day arrived to read my report, my stomach ached. Mrs. Becker called my name, and I slowly stood up. I could feel my face begin to flush a light pink. I began reading my report, my hands shaking slightly, my heart feeling like popcorn popping in my chest, and after reading a few words, my voice cracked. I was mortified. My face became radish red, and I felt the other students staring at me. I couldn't speak. The words weren't coming out of my mouth.

Then, Mrs. Becker came to my rescue.

"It's fine, Mary, you can do it. Just take your time."

I finished without further incident. At the end of my report, I pulled my forty-eight starred American flag out of a brown paper grocery bag and held it up for the students to see, and they thought it was cool. When I was done, I felt such jubilation. I prayed I would never have to do another presentation ever again.

When I began eighth grade, I found out right away that I was going to have to recite the Preamble to the Constitution at the end of the school year in my Social Studies class. I wasn't looking forward to it, but I had the entire school year to practice. I still remember the first couple of lines of the Preamble after forty years.

Christmas Eve Special

Dad

It was 1976 and my family was celebrating Christmas Eve. I was too old to believe in Santa Claus, and my parents were relieved because they did not need to wake up at the crack of dawn anymore to open presents. We began the Danish tradition of opening gifts on Christmas Eve instead of Christmas morning. My father's parents were both born in Denmark and had brought their tradition with them to the U.S. My parents did not get any resistance from their seven children, so we established the new custom in our household.

Our family was sitting in our living room,

chatting happily with one another. We were looking at each other's gifts when our mother announced, "I am off to bed, everyone."

My father stayed on the couch, not joining our mother, which was very unusual. It was great to have some alone time with our dad. He was in rare form that night. I am not sure how many Olympia beers he had consumed, but he was as jolly as Santa on Boxing Day.

I don't know what got into my head, but I thought it would be fun to get our dad to do something silly. I had a thought, but I wasn't sure he would go through with it. I could not resist, so I simply asked, "Dad, why don't you go upstairs and put on Mom's footy pajamas?"

My siblings turned and stared at me, then they smiled. I guess they couldn't believe I would have the guts to ask our father to do a crazy idea, him being a retired Naval Officer.

I kept saying, "It would be so funny. Come on, Dad. I know you can fit into them."

My brothers were getting into it, too, trying to convince our dad. He laughed and said, "Are you all crazy? I am not going to do that." He finally went off to bed wishing us all a Merry Christmas.

We kids stayed up another half hour or so, joking around, completely forgetting what we had tried to get our father to do earlier. Suddenly, we heard our parent's bedroom door open at the top of the stairs, and we all looked up, our eyes popping out of our heads, as we watched our dad strutting down the staircase and into the living room in our mother's footy pajamas. We were all laughing hysterically, including our father. We could barely breathe as tears rolled down our cheeks. I had the presence of mind to run up to my room and grab my camera, taking his picture.

Somewhere in my house is a photo album that contains solid proof that our dad accepted my challenge and put on our mother's pajamas. In the photo, he is standing jauntily, with his hands on his hips, laughing his head off in tartan plaid, lace-trimmed, footy pajamas.

What a wonderful gift we all received that night. It was one of the few times in our lives where our father revealed a fun-loving side of himself, a vulnerable side we rarely saw. It is too bad our mom missed the entire show. She did not believe the story until I got the film developed and showed her the photo of her husband in her pajamas, and she laughed.

Aunt Jane

Aunt Jane – Photo courtesy of Terry Tunnington

My first memory of you, I was three.
Nana Claffy in the hospital, you in your habit.
At the dinner table, I forgot to say please.
You called Mom and Dad Mister and Missus
Rabbit!
My second mother, my respect for you is
immense.
I see you every year, sometimes twice.
You helped me when times were tense.
Listening to me, giving me sound advice.
Sharing much laughter, many tears,
Comforting each other through thick and thin.
Missing our loved ones that had left us over the
years.
Anticipating the next cycle of life to begin.
Your Manhattan accent makes me smile from
ear to ear.
Your reassuring presence makes me feel I have
nothing to fear.

Waiting for the Bus

W hen I think of buses, I think of my Aunt Jane. She is my mom's youngest sister by fourteen years. She taught nursing for twenty-five years at St. Vincent's Hospital in Greenwich Village. As far back as I can remember, she came to visit every summer and Christmas break. Whenever I sat next to her on the couch, she said, "Mimi, we are waiting for the bus." It always made me laugh. I cherished her visits. After my mom died, I flew to New York to spend time with Aunt Jane.

During one such visit, I had recently graduated from middle school in the year of our country's bicentennial. Aunt Jane arrived in June, partly because the nursing school had just let out for the summer and partly because her birthday is on June 10, and my mom's birthday was on June 9. They liked to share their festivities.

My sister, Peggy, had driven down from Auburn for the celebration. She had to work on Monday, so she asked, "Hey, Aunt Jane and Mary, why don't you come back with me? I would love for you to see my new "old" house. Neither of you has been there. I would enjoy your company on the ride home."

"How will we get back to Livermore?" asked Aunt Jane.

"You can take the Greyhound Bus," Peg said.

"Yeah, Aunt Jane, I did that another time with Mark and Chris. It wasn't too bad. We had to transfer buses in Sacramento. It took us about four hours to get home though."

"Sure, Peggy, I would like that," said Aunt Jane. She called Greyhound a few minutes later and bought two tickets from Auburn to Livermore, returning on Wednesday.

We enjoyed our stay with Peggy. She lived in a seventy-five-year-old cottage on an acre of land off Highway 49 in Auburn, California. Peggy got home early from work on Monday and drove us to the American River, a few miles from her house. The water rushed quickly, and I was careful to find a safe spot to swim. It was a cool way to beat the heat of the day.

Our visit went by quickly and before we knew it, Peggy was driving us to the bus depot early Wednesday morning. It wasn't much more than a wooden bench with a Greyhound sign above it. Peg waved goodbye as she drove away in her 1962 VW Bug.

Aunt Jane and I sat for about twenty minutes before the bus arrived. "Hey, Aunt Jane, we are finally waiting for the bus, for real this time." I giggled.

We boarded the bus and only six other people were on it. We rode through all the little towns along Interstate 80 toward Sacramento: Newcastle, Penryn, Loomis, Rocklin, and Roseville. These hamlets were unheard of forty years ago.

After an hour and a half, we were dropped

off at the large bus terminal in Sacramento. We had to find our connecting bus #29 amongst the fifty or so buses at the depot. It was over-whelming to me, but my aunt found it with no problem because she was used to taking buses in New York. Her confidence in traveling made me feel at ease.

We entered bus #29 and found two seats in the middle, on the left-hand side. We sat patiently as the other passengers boarded the bus. The driver announced on the intercom that we would be leaving shortly. He started the engine and was ready to take off when two guys with backpacks began running toward the bus, frantically waving from outside. The driver shook his head and begrudgingly moved the lever to let the two additional passengers inside. The young men thanked the driver, and I could hear by their accents they weren't from the United States. My guess was they were from somewhere in Scandinavia. They walked down the aisle and pulled off their packs and sat on the left side, two rows in front of us.

It didn't take long before the odor of their unwashed bodies began wafting back toward us. It was mid-June and it was already 90 degrees at noon. The AC wasn't working well. I looked at Aunt Jane, and she looked at me with a frown on her face.

I whispered into her ear, "Oh my goodness, Aunt Jane, these guys stink. I wonder how long they are going to be on the bus."

"They are odiferous. Don't worry, I have

something that might help."

She opened her large pocketbook, as she called it, and pulled out a tiny bottle of perfume labeled White Linen. She handed me the bottle and then she pulled two tissues out of a little package of Kleenex and gave one to me.

"Now, Mimi, it is always important to be prepared and carry necessary items on your person." She then took the perfume from me and poured a small amount on the tissue and handed it to me. Then she took the other tissue and repeated the process. She returned the perfume to her pocketbook and showed me how to wrap the tissue around my fingers.

"Mimi, when the body odor gets too overwhelming, hold the tissue up to your nose and sniff it like this." She demonstrated for me.

I looked at my aunt and was amazed at how wise she was. I was grateful to her that day because it was an hour or more before those backpackers disembarked the bus in Stockton. I observed the rest of the passengers breathing a collective sigh of relief after the backpackers exited the bus. I started clapping and the rest of the passengers joined in.

First Car

When I was 17 years old, I wanted a car to get around town. I had a job as an assistant manager at House of Fabrics in Livermore, and I needed a car. I worked 32 hours a week and had two classes at Livermore High, as a senior. I lived two miles from school, and I had been walking or riding my bike since I was in first grade. I didn't make much money, although I think the minimum wage was $2.50 an hour then, so I made about $3.00 an hour. I was on a mission to buy a car, any car.

My sister Katy owned an old Chevy Nova, and she was going to get another car, so she offered to sell the Chevy to me for $400.00. I was thrilled I could afford that. I had never seen the car, so one day, she drove out from San Leandro to show me the car. I couldn't wait. I was so excited. She finally arrived, and to my dismay, there was my future car, and it was so ugly. The top was rusty and had dents in it. The car was an oxidized blue, with Bondo gray on the back right fender. There were rusty holes in the fender. It was a sight. I looked inside the car, and the ripped seats were hidden under seat covers. The coolest thing about the car was a gas pedal in the shape of a foot.

Katy looked at my face, and I think she could tell I was disappointed. She said, "Mary don't knock this car until you drive it." I got in and discovered that it had a manual transmission on the column. I would have to learn how to drive a stick to boot.

So, my brother-in-law Tim, volunteered to teach me. We went out to North Livermore Avenue. I got into the driver seat and Tim showed me how to push in the clutch and so forth. Well, before you know it, I was hauling down the road going 60 mph.

I will never forget that car. I had it until I was twenty-three years old, and I was able to work on it myself. It had a straight-six engine, and I could see through to the ground with the hood up. I sold it to a friend who drove it to Washington State and then to the San Juan Islands, where it finally went to its resting place on Orcas Island.

Backpacking Trip

I n the summer of 1980, I turned eighteen years old and wanted adventure. So I decided to take a backpacking class at Las Positas College. I had always wanted to be in the out-of-doors.

My family was not the outdoorsy type. My lone camping experience was with my parents and two of my brothers when I was eight years old. It consisted of sleeping overnight at Mount Diablo State Park. My parents slept in their red Chevy station wagon while Chris, Mark, and I slept on the ground in sleeping bags. I heard strange noises coming from the table late that night, and I shined my trusty Brownie flashlight toward the rustling. My light flashed into very large raccoon eyes and held tightly in its paws, was a jelly-glazed donut, my favorite. We foolishly left food on the picnic table and during the night, raccoons ate all the donuts from the Donut Wheel! Around 5:00 a.m., blue jays started squawking, finishing the crumbs left by the raccoons. My mother couldn't wait to get home. She was born and raised in a city and by golly, she said, she wasn't going camping ever again.

On the other hand, I had enjoyed my camping experience and loved sleeping outside under the stars. I was envious of the other kids at school who talked about their wonderful fun-filled camping trips with their families, swimming in a lake, making s'mores over a campfire, and hiking in the woods.

Now, at eighteen years of age, I could make my own decision to camp by taking a class and learning how to do it right! Mr. Pole was a coach at Las Positas College and taught the backpacking class. He required a book for the class that explained the appropriate equipment to take on a trip, the correct type of food to bring, and the right clothing to wear. I learned so much about safety and how to hang my food from a tree so the bears couldn't get it. We were going hiking in the Sonora Wilderness, where we might encounter bears, so we needed to be prepared.

After five weeks of learning how to backpack, we were ready to go. About twenty people were in our class. A few couples, a smattering of single young people, and a few middle-aged women and men. Mr. Pole asked four of his "Ultimate Frisbee" players to come on the trip and help. They were all very tall and handsome young men. I was quite pleased to have them along.

I recognized Jean, a girl I knew from high school, who was in my backpacking class. She and I had practiced hiking with our packs on the trails around town a few times. Jean and I were supposed to be hiking partners, but after a few miles into our hiking trip, it became apparent that I was not going to keep up with her five-foot, ten-inch body. So, she started hiking with the Frisbee players. I did feel abandoned, but soon I came across a woman named Patty who was hiking by herself because her husband and two sons had left also. We were about the same height, and we enjoyed each other's company.

Mr. Pole never told us how many miles we would hike that day, but it was an arduous journey. It was very hot and sweat continuously trickled down my back and forehead. Luckily, I wore a baseball cap to keep the sun from blazing on my face. Patty and I checked our maps every so often and wondered how much farther we had to go. The sun was beginning to lower in the west and at dusk, we finally made it to our camp. What a relief! My thirty-five-pound pack had become a lead weight and when I took it off, I felt so light. My shoulders and back throbbed with pain. Patty was also thankful to be at our destination. In the last five miles, she was having a very difficult time walking and wasn't sure she could finish the hike. I encouraged her that she could make it and she did. It was nice to know we weren't the last ones to arrive. Eight hikers had not shown up at the camp, so Mr. Pole sent his four Frisbee players to find them. They came back after dark. Several of the young women and one guy named Scott, about thirty years old, were having a difficult time. The Frisbee players took their packs from them, and they got to walk to camp without all that extra weight.

At the campfire that night, Mr. Pole revealed to us that we hiked twelve miles and climbed

2,000 feet in elevation. No wonder we were all exhausted! Jean and I sleepily put up our tent, but she soon left me to hang out with the Frisbee players. She came back very late. I didn't care because I was exhausted and thought she was foolish for staying up past midnight.

I woke up to the sunlight shining through my tent. I had no idea what time it was, but I got up anyway. Some people were already gathered around the fire. My back and shoulders burned with pain. How was I going to put my pack on again? I tried not to think about it. I made instant oatmeal, and after I ate the steaming hot porridge, I felt much better.

At breakfast, when Mr. Pole told us we were only going to hike four miles that day, we all let out a collective sigh of relief. We broke down camp and were on our way. I found Patty and we walked together. It was so much easier because we were not going up in elevation. We camped by a lake that night. It was a beautiful mountain lake. The cool water felt great on my aching muscles. We heard talk around camp that Scott, the guy who came in late, wasn't doing well. He was weak and coughing up blood. Mr. Pole was trying to decide if Scott's symptoms were serious enough for him to be airlifted out. Scott stayed by the warm campfire that night.

The next morning, we were hiking down in elevation, and Mr. Pole suggested Scott might have altitude sickness. The Frisbee players made a stretcher and carried him to our next camp. It was strange because we had only reached 7,000 feet, which didn't seem too high, but as we descended about 1,000 feet that day, it was enough to make Scott feel better. We were all relieved and had fun celebrating around the campfire that night. The Frisbee players made up limericks about each hiker. Some were funny, and some should have been left unsaid. Especially the one about Jean.

Overall, it was a great experience, and I learned so much about backpacking. I felt physically stronger and wiser from my trip. I kept in touch with Patty and her family for a while, but I never saw Jean again. I continued to camp and backpack into my mid-forties, but now I prefer being in the wilderness in my cabin where I can sleep on my comfy bed.

Mateo

"Mateo, can jou pleaze go wit Esme's frien' Meddy to de BART statshion?" Yolanda yelled upstairs to her son. "Meddy needs to leave in ten minutez. Will jou be ready?"

"Sure, Mom. I will come down," Mateo, her son, yelled back.

A minute later, Mateo came bounding down the stairs.

Esme, Mateo's sister, was my friend from college. "Mateo, this is my friend, Mary. Mary, my brother Mateo."

"Nice to meet you, Mateo," I said, shaking his hand. He was a handsome guy with jet black hair and mustache, warm brown eyes, and a dazzling smile. Not tall, but tall guys never appealed to me that much.

"Nice to meet you, Mary. Where do you live?"

"I live in Livermore. I have to get off at the Bay Fair BART Station where I catch the bus home."

"Oh, okay. I live in Newark. It is a lot easier for me to take the train from there instead of driving my truck to Oakland to visit my parents," he offered.

Esme drove us to the station. We didn't say much in the car. I stood shyly on the train platform trying to make small talk with Mateo. When the train arrived, he ended up sitting next to me, and we talked a little. I got off at Bay Fair and said goodbye wondering if I would ever see him again.

College began and I became very busy with work and my studies. A month later Mateo called me and asked me out on a date. I happily accepted.

Checkout Dive

Mary in the ocean at Monastery Beach, Carmel

I have always loved the ocean. I idolized Jacques Cousteau as a child and watched all his TV programs. My family spent long weekends in Pacific Grove when I was young. We stayed at the Sunset Motel near Asilomar Beach. My siblings and I hopped on the bikes that were provided by the inn and rode down to the water and climbed on the jagged rocks to search for creatures in the tide pools. A few times, I saw scuba divers in the ocean out past the shore and thought, Wow! *I wish I could be a diver and see all the marine animals underwater, just like Jacques Cousteau.*

My dream finally came true. I met my first boyfriend, Mateo, when I was nineteen. On our first date, I found out he was a scuba diver. He encouraged me to take a diving class to get certified. Several months later, I took him up on it.

After my college classes ended in June, I signed up to attend a diving class. It lasted six weeks. I learned about scuba equipment, the science of breathing air underwater, and its dangers. The dive shop had a fifteen-foot-deep pool in the back where students could practice their diving skills with tanks, regulators, fins, masks, weight belts, and buoyancy compensators or BCs, as divers called them. I passed the written test with no problem, but there were other requirements to complete three checkout dives to successfully demonstrate scuba skills in the ocean.

Our first dive was at Stillwater Cove, north of San Francisco. We dove without tanks, which is called "freediving." This helped us get used to wearing wetsuits and other equipment. We students practiced holding our breath and diving down in about twenty feet of water. We learned how to equalize the pressure in our ears while diving.

The other two dives were to be completed in the Monterey Bay. The first two dives were at Breakwater Beach near Cannery Row. It no longer exists because buildings cover the entrance. It was an easy dive in twenty feet of water.

The third dive was completed at Monastery Beach, which is located on Highway 1 on the way to Carmel. This beach is an extremely dangerous place to swim because it is steep. However, on a calm day, it is a great place to scuba dive because the steepness of the beach makes it easier for divers to enter the water quickly and not have to kick out far to see marine life. The Monterey Canyon is located two hundred yards from the shore, and the trench goes down two miles to the bottom of the ocean.

On the day of my third dive, Ellen, my instructor, took eight of us students out to view the underwater canyon. The visibility of the water was about thirty feet, which is great by Northern California standards. The water temperature was 56 degrees, but my wetsuit did a sufficient job keeping me warm. The air temperature was 65 degrees and I was sweating profusely inside my wetsuit. I ambled in my scuba gear through the coarse sand of Monastery Beach to the water. Getting to the ocean was the most difficult part of diving. Once I entered the water, the forty or so pounds I wore became weightless.

My dive buddy, Ron, was a smoker in his late thirties. He huffed and puffed as we entered the water. I was concerned about him and wondered if he was going to complete the dive. We were supposed to stay five feet apart. We were taught to never, ever, dive alone. Your buddy can save your life if your regulator breaks or you run out of air. Once we were out of the surf line, with our BCs inflated, Ellen gave us instructions on sticking together as a group. It was our job to dive no deeper than forty feet. We were to make sure to check our air and depth gauges frequently.

Ellen told us it was time to go under the water. I consulted with Ron and let him know that I was taking the air out of my BC. He did the same. Wetsuits are naturally buoyant, so divers must wear a weight belt to help them sink into the water. Every diver wears a different amount of weight, depending on their body type. I wore twenty-four pounds and Ron only needed to wear fifteen.

Ron and I followed the group of divers west out to the shelf. The regulators helped us breathe air and create little bubbles, which gradually enlarged as they floated to the surface. I could see the sand below and kelp to the left of me, swaying in the water. The sand gave way to dark, jagged rocks. I saw brown rock cod swimming along, with big eyes and spiky fins. Most of them were about six to ten inches long. I saw sea stars stuck to the rocks, like colorful bumper stickers, in shades of red, orange, and yellow. There were deep purple sea urchins, their spikes jutting out from their spherical bodies.

My body had cooled down considerably, especially the exposed skin on my face, which stung in the frigid water. My regulator tasted salty as I clenched down on it with my teeth. The sound of my bubbles was loud, even though my head was covered by the hood of my wetsuit.

When I was under the ocean, I heard clicks, snaps, and bubbles from the other divers and marine mammals in the vicinity.

Ron and I continued to follow Ellen and the other students. Finally, she stopped swimming. She held up her gloved hands in a stopping motion while facing us students. We formed a semicircle around her while we were in forty feet of water. With hand motions, she pointed down with her index fingers. I looked where she was pointing and saw the deepest shade of blue. She motioned for us to come closer to her, and we swam about twenty more feet, and then Ellen stopped us again, pointing down.

We divers were suspended in forty feet of water, each of us a mere speck in the humongous Pacific Ocean. I remember looking down into the abyss, with its variegated shades of blue turning to midnight black, down two miles to where the ocean floor eventually lay. I felt so small and insignificant and that at any moment, I could be pulled down into that dark pit, never to be seen again. My breath quickened and my heart beat faster under my wetsuit. It was terrifying and exciting at the same time.

We hung there for a few more minutes, dangling in the ocean like marionettes without strings, mesmerized by the sight of the canyon. Then Ellen motioned for us to turn around and start heading back to shore. I must say I was relieved. I kicked my legs enthusiastically, my black rubber fins waving up and down through the briny water. It took less time swimming back to shore with the help of the current. Ron and I surfaced in about ten feet of water, filling our BCs with little bits of air to keep us afloat. When I surfaced, I tore the regulator out of my mouth and yelled out, "Woo-hoo! I did it."

I became an official scuba diver that day when Ellen handed me my certificate. I proudly took it from her hand and smiled to myself. If only Jacques could see me now.

Night Dive

As I boarded the boat named *Conception*, I wondered what adventures were in store for me in the next four days. I had been scuba diving for over a year in the frigid waters of Northern California and was looking forward to diving in the balmy waters of the Channel Islands in Southern California. Mateo was joining me.

I was ecstatic to dive off a boat for the first time. I would not have to gear up at my car and trudge through the hot sand like I normally did in Monterey Bay. The crew informed us that there would be two dives a day off the boat. We had to let the divemaster know of our plans so he would know how many divers were in the water to prevent anyone from getting left behind. We were going to motor out to the farthest island the first day and work our way back to Santa Barbara over the next four days.

"The last dive will be at night," said the Divemaster.

"A night dive?" I said frowning. "Do we have to do it?"

"No, you don't. It's optional, but it's usually the highlight for most divers. I recommend that you take advantage of this opportunity."

The next three days, I was in heaven, suiting up in equipment with crewmembers helping me put the tank on my back. The water was about 65 degrees, much warmer than the 55 degrees I was used to. The water was much clearer, too, the visibility up to sixty feet.

I saw many Garibaldi, the California state fish. They were the color of California poppies and curious as kittens. It was as if they knew it was against the law to catch them. They were constantly swimming up to me and nibbling on my wetsuit. I petted them with my neoprene gloves. I thought they were adorable creatures.

The following day we did our deepest dive, 100 feet down a rock wall. We could only stay down there for ten minutes and then start to slowly come up ten feet at a time. The rock wall held all kinds of marine life. There were scallops with their bright orange lips, cobalt nudibranchs, hundreds of sea stars in a rainbow of colors, brain coral and Sheepshead fish and Rock Cod. I even saw a Lemon Shark. What a spectacular dive. I was content.

It finally came the day I needed to decide. *Should I go on the night dive or skip it?* I had to be sure. I didn't want to get in the water that night and freak out. Mateo tried to talk me into it.

"Come on, Mary, you need to do it. I did it last year and I had no problems."

"Really? Well, it's so dark down there. I'm scared."

"Tonight, the moon's almost full and it will give us some light. Also, I have a big watertight flashlight to help us see where we are going. Come on, you'll be fine."

"Okay, I guess I'll do it. But you better stay close to me. Promise?"

"Sure, I promise. You won't regret it, Mary."

The dive was to take place at ten o'clock. The crew wanted it to be nice and dark for us divers to get the ultimate experience. I suited up slowly wondering if I was making the right decision. I stood by the back of the boat waiting to jump into the ocean.

"Come on, Mary, it'll be fine. I will jump in first and turn the light on and then you jump in next, okay?" said Mateo.

"Okay, go ahead. I'll come right after you."

Mateo jumped in and turned the light down into the water. I took a deep breath and jumped in near him. We then put our regulators in our mouths and began to empty our BCs of air. Mateo grabbed my gloved hand and off we went down into the ocean.

It was incredible to be in the ocean at night. The fish floating suspended in the water appeared to be asleep. I looked for lobsters, which are active at night. I saw one in a small cave, and when Mateo tried to grab it, the lobster scooted away using its powerful tail to escape. I was enjoying myself, forgetting my fear.

Mateo stopped me and pointed up to the surface. I could see the moon through thirty feet of water. I was spellbound. I felt alive and privileged to witness such a sight.

Suddenly the flashlight went out. I turned my head quickly to see if I could see Mateo. I could see a dark shape next to me and Mateo grabbed my hand to reassure me. We sat in the water, looking at the moon while being gently rocked by the surge.

As we hovered transfixed by the moon, something bumped me from behind. I turned abruptly to see what had hit me. I pulled on Mateo's arm to alert him. I could sense that he was trying to turn on the light, when a big animal swooshed by us again. Still the light was out. I was beyond terrified, breathing quickly, the bubbles streaming from my regulator in rapid succession.

I grabbed Mateo by the arm shaking him, trying to pull him up to the surface. He seemed to understand what I was trying to do, and we began to move up slowly. Even in thirty feet of water, we were not supposed to ascend quickly. It was important to let the air out of our lungs slowly and not hold our breath. Mateo was the more experienced diver and took control of the situation. He kept us at a steady pace. I could feel him try to switch on the light, but it wasn't working.

When we surfaced, I was so relieved. I could see the dive boat about twenty yards away. I ripped out my regulator and yelled to Mateo, "What the hell was that?"

"I don't know, Mary, I couldn't see it."

"Was it a shark?" I stammered.

"I don't know."

Suddenly the animal hit my fins. I screamed, "What is it?"

I kicked to the boat as quickly as I could.

Mateo yelled to the crewmember, "Hey, there is an animal in the water. I think it's after us."

The divemaster must have heard Mateo because a bright spotlight shone in the water around us. At first, I saw nothing, and then, out of the corner of my eye, I saw something rapidly swimming towards us. "Mateo, it's coming towards us!"

As it came into the beam of the light, I saw what had been tormenting us. It was a harbor seal. It whizzed past us and then a few seconds later, another one swam up to us, surfaced, and looked at us as if laughing and saying, "Tag, you're it." The seal swam away, bubbles trailing behind it.

"Oh, thank God. They're seals," I exclaimed. Then I began to laugh hysterically and so did Mateo.

"Wow, Mary, I hate to admit it, but I was scared too. I thought it was a great white shark."

Leaving Home

I left home in 1983 at the age of twenty-one. I had had a tough year and needed a change. I had been going to Cal State Hayward as a Speech Pathology major. That spring, I was having problems with my boyfriend, Mateo, and feeling very stressed out. I began seeing a counselor at the college to help me sort through some issues. She was very helpful and told me that I should take a break from school. I had been very intent on finishing college in four years. She told me that I could always go back if I wanted to. I was having a dilemma about my major. I knew that I was going to have to get a master's degree to get a job as a speech pathologist, and I wasn't going to be able to work because the program was very difficult. I was putting myself through school as a server and living at home. My parents did not charge me rent while I was going to college. They did not pay for any of my college tuition or books. They told me that they couldn't pay for the seven of us to go to college, so they wouldn't pay anything for me. It was a shame because I was the only one who was going to college at the time.

I decided to withdraw from school in April and it was so freeing. I called my friend Sandi who was living in the San Juan Islands in Washington and asked her if I could come up and she said yes. I broke up with Mateo, quit my job, and got on a plane, within a week of dropping out of school. It was quite a whirlwind experience, and I was extremely excited about the change. I didn't know how long I was going to be there, so I bought a one-way ticket. I told my parents I was leaving, and they didn't seem to care one way or another.

When I told Mateo I was leaving, he was upset and asked me when I was coming back, and I told him I didn't know. He had told me a month before that he wanted to see other people and I told him that it was "all me" or "no me." It felt good to tell him I was leaving and seeing him sad for once.

It took three plane rides to get to Orcas Island, and it was breathtaking. The sky was crystal clear, and I could see the beautiful blue lakes and white snowcapped mountains. I flew into Seattle and spotted the Space Needle. I then took a commuter plane to Whidbey Island and then a four-seater to Orcas Island. Flying over the San Juan Islands was spectacular. The sun glinted off the water and the green trees covered the little islands like heads of broccoli. It is one of the most beautiful places I have ever been.

I was early and Sandi wasn't there to pick me up. The Orcas Island airport consisted of a very small building and a short asphalt landing strip. Luckily, the shack had a phone, and I called Sandi and told her that I had arrived early. I stood waiting in the field looking at the majestic trees surrounding me. She drove up in her little blue Toyota truck with a smile on her face.

We celebrated being together and had a wonderful dinner. Sandi said, "I am moving to Incline Village in three weeks."

"Why didn't you tell me on the phone before I flew to the island?"

"You would never have come to the island, and you needed a break."

"You are right."

I had been open to living up there if the situation presented itself, but it wasn't meant to be.

Mateo called me about a week after I had left for the island. I told him that I would be coming back in two weeks. He told me he had a two-week vacation and that he would come and get me. I was very moved and thought he really loved me. So the two weeks after he picked me up in Seattle, we camped in British Columbia and had a wonderful time.

I moved in with Sandi in August because she broke up with her boyfriend. Our other friend, Claire, had found a house for rent in Sunol, and we all moved into the 100-year-old house. Claire managed a restaurant in Milpitas called the Big Yellow House. She gave Sandi and me jobs as servers. We had a lot of fun together in that house for the next couple of years until I married Mateo in 1985.

In a Fog

I gave myself permission to take a break from college to re-examine my life. I had a few unrewarding jobs and was looking for a more meaningful position. While I scanned the newspaper, searching the want ads for an interesting job, I absently munched on a poppy seed Costco muffin. It's strange how favorite foods can comfort us in life's transitions.

I kept seeing "Experience needed" in the job listings. I came upon an interesting post, "Optometric assistant needed for a busy optometry office. Looking for an energetic person. Will train."

How refreshing. A job where someone will train me. This is just what I'm looking for. This will give me some hands-on experience that I need.

I called the number from the ad and spoke to a woman named Vicky. She had a soft, kind voice. "Can you please come in tomorrow at 10:00 a.m. for an interview?"

"Yes, I can. Thank you so much, Vicky. I will see you tomorrow."

I hung up the phone. I had a good feeling about this job and hoped Vicky would hire me. I tingled all over with anticipation.

The name of the optometry office was Fremont Optometric Group. It was located on the bustling corner of Fremont and Stevenson

Boulevard in Fremont. I carefully dressed for my interview: silk blouse, tweed skirt, two-inch heels, and suntan pantyhose, standard interview apparel in 1983.

I walked into the office at 9:55 a.m. and pressed the buzzer next to the small, frosted window. The receptionist quietly slid open the glass and smiled. "Hello, may I help you?" Her nametag read Kathy.

"Hi, Kathy. My name is Mary Hansen. I am here for an interview with Vicky."

"Oh, yes. I will let her know you have arrived." She slid the window closed.

I sat down and waited while Muzak played an old Burt Bacharach tune. I grabbed a *People* magazine to pass the time. I didn't have to wait long before a petite woman with short, blond hair opened the door to the back office.

"Hi. You must be Mary. I'm Vicky. We spoke on the phone yesterday."

"Yes. It's nice to meet you." I shook her hand gently and smiled.

Vicky led me down a short, wood-paneled hallway to an empty examination room, which contained an eye chart on the wall and various machines to examine eyes. I smelled the sharp scent of rubbing alcohol. Another woman with short, brunette hair sat on a swivel stool. She stood up and introduced herself.

"Hi, Mary. My name is Martha. I am the assistant office manager. Vicky and I are both going to interview you. She is the office manager."

I was feeling a bit overwhelmed with the two of them in the tiny exam room, but I took a deep breath and smiled. *Just be yourself. You're going to do well.*

Vicky asked about my education and job experience. I told her I had six previous jobs, three at restaurants for the same Big Yellow House chain, and three clerk/cashier jobs in retail. I told them I wanted a rewarding job.

After about fifteen minutes of questions and answers, Vicky looked at Martha and they both nodded to one another and grinned.

"Martha and I would like to welcome you to our office. The job is yours if you want it. We believe you will fit in quite well with the rest of the staff."

"Yes, I want it. Thank you. I didn't think I would find out this quickly."

"You are exactly the person we were looking for. When can you start?"

"Whenever you want me to. How about tomorrow?"

"Sure, that would be great. We would like you to work from 9:00 a.m. to 6:00 p.m. Monday through Friday."

The next morning, I arrived punctually and began my training with Vicky. She oversaw training the back-office staff who performed preliminary eye tests on patients and helped them select frames, while Martha trained the front-office staff, which included the receptionist and insurance billers. They needed me in the back office.

I learned quickly, and after a few months, our office moved to a larger location on Fremont Boulevard. I worked for three optometrists: Drs. Tsujimoto, Gin, and Chew. My favorite doctor was Dr. Tsujimoto. He was kind, patient, and extremely intelligent. He always ran late because he was thorough with his patients and listened to them.

I was polite with the patients and loved helping them pick out their frames. I was quite good at finding the correct shape and color of eyeglasses to fit each person's unique characteristics. I enjoyed my job. I seemed to fit in well with the group of office personnel. But as our office grew, so did the number of employees. I began to train the optometric assistants after Vicky hired them.

I worked there for two years, and the environment began to deteriorate. We had gone from six office workers to twelve, and they were all women. I was twenty-three and many of the young women were about twenty years old that were hired. Most of us got along, but soon the girls began talking behind each other's backs, and it was strained at work. Petty arguments and resentment began to change the office staff.

We wore uniforms at work, white pants, white shoes, and a medical office top of various designs. A few of the girls were getting more and more flashy shirts and jewelry. They were wearing lots of makeup, and their hairdo began to get bigger and bigger. It got to be such a competitive work environment, I didn't feel that

I fit in anymore. We employees called our office F.O.G. for fun, but I felt that I was working in a cold fog of meaningless gossip. I felt as though I was back in middle school trying to fit in, and I didn't want any part of it. I decided to look for another job, one with more mature employees.

I looked in the want ads again and found a listing for an ophthalmic assistant for two ophthalmologists in town. I was interviewed by the senior doctor and was hired on the spot. I had similar duties to that of the previous job, but the employees were women in their forties to sixties. It was a much calmer and cohesive group of women. I worked there until I gave birth to my first child. When I reflect on my experiences in life, I realize that I have always gotten along better with people older than myself.

Birth Sisters

Katy and Mary

In May of 1986, I suspected that I was pregnant, so I took a home pregnancy test, and sure enough, the plus sign turned blue. I was twenty-four years old, barely a woman myself. I didn't know about babies since I was the youngest of seven children. I hardly babysat because all the kids in my neighborhood were my age or went to school with my older siblings.

Still, I was ecstatic. I couldn't wait to tell my family members, especially my sister, Katy, who had three sons of her own. I admired her very much. Katy was a wonderful, attentive, and loving mother. She went above and beyond for her children.

At the time, Katy lived in San Leandro and I in Fremont. I called her right away.

"Hi Katy. I have some great news. I'm pregnant."

"Really? Wow, that's great, Mary. I am so happy for you."

I hung up the phone and felt relief that I had a sister who was going to help support me through my pregnancy. She and I had always been close.

Katy called me a week later. "Hi, Mary. I have some news to share with you."

"Really? What is it?"

"I am pregnant too."

"You are? That's great. We can be pregnant together. When are you due?"

"I am due January 31st. How about you, Mary?"

"I'm due February 8th. Wow, our due dates are only eight days apart."

I was overjoyed that we were going to share our pregnancies. During the next several months, I called Katy with all sorts of questions. She was a seasoned mother, and I took advantage of her expertise.

The weeks and the months flitted by and Katy and I grew larger. Christmas came and went and in January, Katy's doctor scheduled her for a C-section, January 23rd. We both figured I would have my baby sometime around February 8th, since most first babies are late. Katy wanted a girl, and I wished for one too.

On Friday, January 23rd, Katy went to the

hospital early that morning for her surgery. A few hours later, I called my mom from work during my lunch break, and she told me that Katy had a girl. We were all so happy and excited for my sister.

After I got off work, I went home and ate a quick dinner with Mateo, and I drove to Kaiser Hospital in Hayward to see Katy and her baby girl. Back then, visitors couldn't go into the maternity ward unless they were a parent or grandparent. The hospital had a covered walkway outside the maternity ward. Visitors could walk out and look at the babies and their mothers through the hospital room windows. I called Katy to tell her that I would come to see her around 7:00 p.m. I was so excited to see my brand new niece. I found Katy's window, but she was in bed, recovering from her C-section. Tim brought the baby to the window. He was a proud father showing me his beautiful baby girl. Wow what a wonderful day it was. I blew a kiss to Katy through the glass and she beamed with joy and blew one back.

That weekend, I called Katy at the hospital to chat. She decided to name her daughter Katelyn because it was like her name. My sister had come from a long line of Kathleen's: my mother, grandmother, and great-grandmother.

I went to work the next few days feeling jubilant. But by Wednesday, I felt a little peculiar, a bit more tired than usual. I got home from work at the eye doctor's office at 6:15 p.m. I stretched out in my recliner and put up my feet. I told Mateo I was feeling strange, so he cooked dinner. After a half hour, I got up to go to the bathroom, and I felt a warm trickle drip down my leg.

"Oh, I think my water broke."

"Are you sure, Mary?"

"Well, it didn't gush, but I felt water come out of me."

"Okay, let's wait and see what happens in the next hour."

Mateo was a firefighter and had helped deliver a few babies, so I felt secure with him around. Within ten minutes of my water breaking, my contractions began. I called the hospital and told the nurse what was going on. She told me when the contractions got to five minutes apart, to go to the hospital. She asked me when my due date was and I told her February 8th, and it was only January 27th.

Around 1:00 a.m., I timed my contractions, and they were five minutes apart. Mateo grabbed my overnight bag, and I awkwardly climbed into the car. He drove me to Kaiser. I was admitted and wheeled up to labor and delivery.

My labor room was the size of a broom closet. I labored for several hours, and I was having strong, painful contractions and crushed Mateo's hand with each one. He looked exhausted, so I told him to go take a break. I asked him to check to see if my sister was still at the hospital.

The next thing I knew, Katy walked into my

room and I began to cry. She came to my bedside and gently held my hand. She stayed with me for a few hours so that my husband could take a nap. Having Katy next to me brought me such comfort. Her calming nature was exactly what I needed during that difficult time.

"Mary, it breaks my heart to see you in such pain. I wish I could take it away."

"Katy, just having you here with me has helped me so much. Thank you."

I will never forget Katy's loving eyes and the compassion she showed me that day. She distracted me, and I appreciated her tenderness in my time of need. I was sorry to see her leave, but it was time for her to take Katelyn home.

Alana Maria

Alana Maria

On January 28, 1987, the surgeon performed a C-section to deliver my baby. The surgeon announced, "You have a baby girl." My heart soared. I wanted a daughter so much and I got one. It was 10:11 pm. I had been in labor for twenty-six hours. I desperately wanted to hold my little girl, but I couldn't because my arms were strapped to boards with an IV in one arm and blood pressure cuff on the other. Then, after the doctor sewed me up, I had to go to recovery.

When the recovery room nurse woke me up, I asked for my daughter. Then the nurse said I had to wait until I got to my room. Later, an orderly wheeled me to my room, and again I asked for my baby girl. The nurse told me I would have to wait until morning. I was so angry. I wanted to hold my baby. How could they keep her from me? It was two o'clock in the morning and the nurse told me to rest and gave me some pain medication and I fell asleep.

Finally, at 5:30 a.m., a nurse came in and woke me up and told me she would be bringing my baby soon. I was exhausted and extremely sore, but I sat up in anticipation. I would get to hold my child, my girl, and my hope for the future. When the nurse wheeled her in, I began to cry. She lifted her out of the clear plastic hospital bassinet, and I saw a shock of black hair. As I reached my arms out for her, I instantly fell in love. I held my girl gently in my arms, kissing her head, nose, ears, fingers, and cheeks. I'm not sure what the nurse thought or if she had seen this a hundred times before, but I was unaware of anything else. I proceeded to unwrap the blanket that kept my daughter warm; I had to see her entire body. She was so perfect, so beautiful, my daughter. I then nursed my baby girl, and we were bonded forever.

As I held this child in my arms, I looked at her, trying to find the perfect name for her. Names are very important to me, and I wanted to make sure it fit her. It took me two days to name her, and the nurses were getting impatient with me, coming in a few times a day with the birth certificate form. I finally decided on Alana Maria. Alana, meaning beautiful girl child in Irish and Maria, Spanish for Mary, after me.

Mom and Dad,
I Need Your Advice

Dad, Katelyn, Mom, and Alana

I t was Christmas Eve, 1988. I was heading to Livermore to Colleen's home to celebrate the holiday with my siblings and parents. Mateo was working at the fire station, so I dressed Alana in her scarlet corduroy pinafore and brushed her wavy brunette hair and topped it with a bow. Alana would be turning two years old in a month.

I strapped Alana in her car seat, in our Plymouth Voyager minivan, along with several wrapped presents. Since I had six siblings decided ten years ago to draw names, so we wouldn't spend all our time and money buying Christmas presents for one another. It was one of the smartest decisions our family made.

I lived in Fremont, which was a twenty-five-minute drive to Colleen's house. I always enjoyed the drive there. I took the 680 freeway and got off on Highway 84, which was windy but took me through the gorgeous emerald rolling hills to my hometown. As soon as I descended onto 84, into the Livermore Valley, I felt a sense of well-being. It was where I belonged. It was familiar and safe. But today I had an issue that weighed upon my mind.

Colleen always had her house decorated to the max. She had multicolored lights on the outside of her house, which greeted me with warmth as I drove up to the curb. The winter sun hung low in the sky. I was eager to see my family. Since I had married in 1985 and moved to Fremont, I rarely saw my extended family. I was very lonely in Fremont with Mateo working 24-hour shifts at the firehouse. Since I gave birth to Alana, I decided to stay home and care for her.

I unstrapped Alana from her car seat and helped her down out of the van. She looked adorable in her Christmas dress. I wore a dress of a lovely impressionistic print in navy, fuchsia, green, and lavender. The dress was smooth and silky and draped over my distended belly. I knocked on the door and ten seconds later, Colleen opened it with a cheerful greeting of, "Hello Merry Christmas. Boy Mare, you're showing a lot already."

"I know I sure wasn't this big at five months with Alana."

"Come on in. You two are the first to arrive.

P.J. is looking forward to playing with all of his cousins."

I held Alana's little hand as we walked into the house. The Christmas tree was to the right in the living room, strewn with colored glass ornaments and decorated to perfection. A little town of painted ceramic buildings lay under the tree on top of soft fleeced snow. A model train surrounded the town and tree.

I arrived at 4:00 p.m. The next to arrive was my sister, Peggy, brother, Pat, with my mom and dad. My brother, Chris, and his wife Ann, and their one-year-old son, Joel, came next. Mark, his wife Karla, and their two girls, Megan, four, and Chelsea, three years old. Katy and her brood always came last. They lived in San Leandro, thirty-five minutes away. She had four children: Joshua, 7, Caleb, 6, Dawson, 3, and Katelyn, almost two years old. She and Alana were born in January five days apart. My sister, Colleen, and her husband, Conley, had one child, P.J., who was eight years old at the time. Twenty-two members of the Hansen clan gathered to celebrate Christmas.

It was a joy to watch the nine cousins. Five boys and four girls interact with one another. Thank goodness Colleen had a large home. My parents always sat in the same spot on the couch, smoking their cigarettes, Tareyton 100s. I hated their habit and tried many times over the years to get them to quit, but they never did.

As I looked at my parents, I felt nervous. There was something I wanted to discuss with them, but was this the right time to ask? I didn't get to see them much in person, so with courage and a deep breath, I approached them. Colleen was sitting on one side of our mother and Mark was sitting next to our father, all on the couch. I sat on the edge of the coffee table in front of the four of them while the children and the rest of the family chatted with one another in small clusters.

"Hey, Mom and Dad, I need your advice."

"Sure, Mimi. What's up?" Dad said in his deep baritone.

"Well, it's kind of hard to talk about."

"Mimi, you can talk to us about it," my mom responded.

"Well, I think I am going to have a boy this time. I am much larger than when I was pregnant with Alana," I said hesitantly.

"Go on," said my dad.

"Since I think I am having a boy, it got me contemplating. I have been reading a lot of new information and it seems pediatricians are now recommending not to circumcise boy babies and I want to know what you both think. You had three sons. I want to know what opinions you have so that it can help me make my decision."

Before either of my parents could respond, Colleen blurted out, "Uncircumcised men are disgusting and dirty."

Our mother took a puff of her cigarette and slowly turned her head towards my sister and said, "Well, Colleen, your father isn't circumcised."

With that, Colleen screwed up her face and

no words came out of her mouth. Mark and I looked at Colleen with horrified faces.

I asked, "Mom, since Dad wasn't circumcised, why did you have it done with Pat, Chris, and Mark?"

"Well, when they were born, that is what was done. I didn't question it. So, it is up to you, Mimi."

"Well, Dad, since you are not circumcised, what is your opinion?"

We looked at our dad as he took a puff of his cigarette, anticipating his response. He said, "It helps with extension."

Mark and I began to laugh so hard, tears streamed down our cheeks. Colleen and my mom joined in too, and that was the end of the discussion.

Babies + College = Sleepless Nights

Amando

When my daughter, Alana, was a year and a half old, I decided to go back to college to finish my degree. In the summer of 1988, I began taking one class at Cal State Hayward. I took archaeology, which has always been a favorite subject of mine. I had gone to the class for three weeks when I found out I was pregnant with my second child.

I decided that having another baby was not going to deter me. My mind was made up and I was going to finish. I had a year and a half to go, so I planned on working hard. That fall, I signed up for a full load of classes. I wanted to be a teacher, so I chose human development as my major.

I was due to have my baby in the middle of April the following year. I had morning sickness, but it was ironic because I usually felt sick at dinnertime. So, it worked out well since I took classes in the morning. I picked my daughter up from the university daycare at 1:00 p.m. and tried my best to keep her awake until we got home. If she slept for just five minutes in the car, she would be awake for the rest of the afternoon and evening. It was crucial that I keep her awake because I needed a nap too. I would ask Alana questions or have her sing songs to keep her from falling asleep.

I was getting large fast, and the doctor thought I might be having twins. After an ultrasound, I found out it was only one baby. I had to get up at night to go to the bathroom, but it wasn't too bad. I was still getting enough sleep. Around my seventh month of pregnancy, I was getting very large and very uncomfortable. I had gained 20 pounds at that point, but it was all baby and I felt like a hippopotamus. I would wake up at night because my belly ached. I used pillows to support my belly and back. I was not getting enough sleep. I was cranky and lethargic. Meanwhile, I was still going to college and sitting from 8:00 a.m. to 12:45 p.m. every day with short breaks between classes. My tailbone began to ache because of the weight of the baby and the constant sitting.

The quarter ended, thankfully, in the middle of March, and I took the spring quarter off to have my baby. By the middle of April, I was huge and could hardly walk. I had trouble breathing as I lay on the examination table at the doctor's office. I kept having labor pains, but I was not dilating. Finally, my doctor ordered another ultrasound to check the weight and size of the baby. The doctor who performed the ultrasound specialized in predicting the size of a fetus said, "Mary, your baby is measuring over ten pounds and its head is measuring almost 14 inches in diameter. I would recommend a caesarian section because you are not a big woman."

The next day, I was scheduled to have the surgery and when the doctor pulled the baby out, he said, "Oh, he is big. You have a big boy." I was not surprised. As the doctor was stitching me up, the OR nurse told me that my son weighed 10 lbs. 11ozs. I couldn't believe it. I thought about all the pain I had been going through and it made sense.

I named my son Amando which means Beloved of God, and I quickly nicknamed him Mondo-Man, because he was by far the biggest baby in the nursery. He looked like he was three months old. Amando had a full head of black hair and big beautiful hazel eyes. Seriously, he looked like a miniature linebacker for the Raiders. He had to wear medium-sized diapers as a newborn.

I had many sleepless nights with my newborn. I was breastfeeding my son, so it was always me who got up at night. I was hoping by September he would be sleeping through the night because I was going back to college, but I wasn't so lucky. He kept waking up two to three times a night, and I was exhausted during class. I was desperate to do anything to get a good night's sleep. Thankfully, Amando was a very happy and content baby during the daytime hours and was a pleasure to be around.

As a senior in college, I was required to write a research paper to graduate. I was going to choose, "How to write a children's book," but I changed my mind. I decided to write a paper on "How to get your child to sleep through the night." Databases were just in their infancy, but I collected as much research material as I could about children and sleep. Dr. Ferber, who researched children's sleep, wrote the most thorough information. I decided to use his method on Amando and collect data to write a paper about our experience.

The basic Ferber method to get a child to sleep through the night is this: when the child wakes up during the night, go into the room, reassure the child with your voice, but do not pick him up. Keep doing this every ten minutes, then fifteen minutes, and so on. Eventually, the child will fall back to sleep. If you have ever been through this, you know it is pure torture. But after three nights of this routine, Amando finally slept through the night. There were a couple of little blips after that, but it worked. I was like a different person. I was much more pleasant to be around. I know I was a more patient mother and wife.

I wrote the research paper on "How to get your child to sleep through the night" and received an "A" on the paper. It was published by the Human Development Department and put in a collection of research papers by students. It was very rewarding at my college graduation to have my son, Amando, with me. Even though he was one year old, he helped me graduate from college. I feel as though we made that journey together. Today, my Mondo-Man is six feet tall and a UC Berkeley graduate of mechanical engineering. He is a very kind and intelligent young man, and I am proud to call him my son.

Ivan Kovacs

I n 1988 I decided to go back to college to finish getting my Bachelor's degree. I was twenty-six at the time with a toddler, and I felt old compared to other students. I decided to change my original major from speech pathology to human development. The main reason, truthfully, is that I needed fewer classes to get my degree. I also liked the curriculum of the human development department. Psychology, sociology, and anthropology courses made up the bulk of the major's requirements, and I enjoyed learning these subjects.

I started my major classes in the fall and gradually began to meet the professors of the human development department. Six main professors gave lectures during a semester, and we were required to choose one of them as our advisor for the next two years.

During my junior year, I got to know each of the professors from my classes, and I felt that Ivan Kovacs was the right advisor for me. He was the oldest professor in the department, and I felt the wisest. He was kind and patient and had an interesting background. He was originally from Budapest, Hungary. He was about five feet, six inches tall with salt and pepper hair. He had a stocky build and a swarthy complexion and wore silver wire-framed glasses. He reminded me of my father. Ivan had a slight Slavic accent and a voice that was pleasant to listen to during a long lecture.

One day, during one of Ivan's lectures, a student asked him where he came from. I was pleased that Ivan shared his life story with us. He grew up in Hungary and was a student at the University of Budapest where he received his BA and MA degrees in Special Education. While Ivan was a student, he became dissatisfied with his government and the restrictions in education and freedom of expression. The Cold War had its adverse effects on people behind the Iron Curtain that was frustrating and confining.

Ivan was in his early twenties when he decided to make the difficult decision to leave his country and go to the United States. His parents were older, and they gave him their blessing to leave Hungary. Ivan made his plans, got his fake passport, and carefully orchestrated his escape. He needed to make it to the Austrian border and sneak through undetected.

It was winter and Ivan had to hitch a ride with strangers to get as close to the border as he could. He then had to trudge through deep snow and cut through a barbed wire fence without being caught.

Ivan eventually made his way to the United States and lived in Michigan for a while, acquiring his Ph.D. in Human Development in 1967. He met and married his wife and came to California in 1970. He applied for a position at Cal State Hayward and worked there for 30 years. Ivan is currently an Emeritus Professor for the university.

During my senior year of college, Ivan advised me regarding my papers and decisions concerning my classes. One day, as I was speaking to him about my future in education, I said, "Ivan, do you think I could get a Master's degree in education?" He said, "Mary, why stop at a Master's degree. You should get a Ph.D." I looked at him and got tears in my eyes and said, "Ivan, do you really think that I could get a Ph.D.?" And he said, "Mary, you are intelligent and have so much to offer people."

I left his office that day with an entirely new perspective about myself. A professor actually thought that I could accomplish something that I hadn't contemplated, acquiring a Ph.D.! No one in my life up to that point ever encouraged me or supported me to such an extent. My parents never even encouraged me to go to college, let alone to get an advanced degree. I was awestruck and amazed and felt like I was walking on clouds. I so much appreciated that Ivan saw so much potential in me.

I haven't gotten a Ph.D., and I don't know if I ever will, but Ivan helped me realize I have the power to do whatever I set my mind to and he inspired me to have faith in myself. I will be forever grateful to him.

Amando at four

When Amando was a baby, he periodically got fevers and looked very sick. I brought him to the pediatrician's office to get him checked out and the doctor always told me it was a virus that will go away in time. I was twenty-six years old at that time and didn't have much experience with doctors or sick babies.

When Amando was three years old, we went camping up near Ukiah at a place called Lake Mendocino. I also had my daughter, Alana, with me, who was five at the time. We arrived at the lake and set up camp, our dome tent, ice chest, and Coleman stove. The first night at camp was fine, but the next morning, Amando was not feeling well. His color was off. His skin had a yellowish tint instead of his normal warm caramel tone. I had noticed that Amando had woken up with a dry diaper. Then it hit me. I said, "Mondo, does it hurt when you go pee-pee?"

He said, "Yes, Mommy, it hurts really bad!"

I thought, "He must have a bladder infection." I told Mateo that we had better pack up and leave. Amando vomited and had a high fever. It was clear he was very sick.

We drove back home, which was a three-hour drive, and I couldn't wait to get there. I made a short-notice appointment for Amando at the Kaiser clinic in Fremont, which is where we lived at the time. For some reason, Mateo took Amando to the appointment, which was very unusual. When he told the doctor that we thought Amando had a bladder infection, the doctor was skeptical, but he took a urine sample, and Amando's urine was cloudy with white blood cells. The doctor said Amando had a kidney infection and put him on antibiotics. He also requested several other tests: an ultrasound of his kidneys, a kidney function, and VCUG, which would check his bladder and ureter function.

I was very upset. Here was my poor little boy, only three years old, having to go through all this testing, but I wanted to find out what was going on. With each test, it was revealed how sick Amando was. He was finally diagnosed with vesicoureteral reflux. It meant that Amando's ureters didn't work properly, and the urine would back up into his kidneys every time he voided. The VCUG test revealed that his ureters were distended and had no muscle tone to them. The urine went straight up to the kidneys and his bladder never fully emptied.

As a result, Amando had been getting kidney infections since he was born, and his right kidney was permanently scarred and only had ten percent function. A pediatric nephrologist put him on antibiotics. He told me that children eventually grow out of this condition because as they grew taller the ureters would grow and stretch. So, I went along with this information, but I wasn't convinced.

I did as much research as possible on this condition. I read medical journals and articles on the subject. I found out that it would not go away if the ureters were severely impaired. A year went by and Amando had another infection. I was so upset because every time he had an infection, the kidney could be scarred more. I went to his doctors and told them that I felt Amando needed something more than antibiotics until he was twenty and this was not going to be acceptable to me. The pediatrician told me that I was overreacting and that I should go down and make an appointment with a psychiatrist. I walked out on him. I was offended and frustrated and very angry.

I went home and called a friend who was an RN, and she gave me a patient assistant number

I could call and get the help I needed for Amando. Within minutes, Amando's pediatrician called me and to ask what I wanted. I told him I wanted a different pediatric nephrologist, and I wanted a second opinion at Stanford. So, I got Amando's records from Kaiser and made an appointment with Stanford, and I got an appointment with another doctor at Kaiser. I had to pay $400 for the Stanford appointment, but I didn't mind. I was going to do everything available to get the right care for my son.

We saw the Stanford doctor and she said, Amando needs another test, a laparoscopy of his bladder and ureters to determine the right course of action. Depending on the result, he may have to have surgery."

We sent the report to Kaiser. We took Amando to the new Kaiser doctor, and he said that he didn't believe the previous doctor looked at Amando's films, that if he had, he would have requested surgery several years ago. I felt validated and respected that day.

A month later, Amando had the surgery and it was a success. I brought him to a new pediatrician to have a recheck after the surgery. I heard a knock on the door to the examination room and in walked the pediatrician who had told me to make a psychiatric appointment. I just looked at him in disbelief. He said, "I heard that Amando's surgery was needed and it was successful."

"Yes, it was," I replied.

"It was good that you went with your

instincts and pursued what you thought was right."

"Yes, I am glad I did what was best for my son."

He put out his right hand, but I didn't want to shake it. I was still so angry with this man, but I needed to be the better person so I shook his hand. I'm glad I never saw him again.

Amando has done great. After the surgery, he grew eight inches in two years. The condition had prevented him from growing normally. He is now six feet tall. I would do anything for my children. I became a much stronger person because of this injustice to my son. It changed my life and my son's. I am so thankful that I pursued the matter and my son is healthy today.

Colton's First Shot

Colton

Years ago, when Colton was two, unusual circumstances surrounded his first shot. It all began one night when he woke up crying, which was strange because Colton had slept through the night since he was six weeks old. I was worried. *What could be wrong?*

It was a frigid night after the holiday season when I was awakened by Colton's cries. I rubbed my sleepy eyes and threw back the warm covers, reluctantly getting out of bed. I was wearing a long white flannel nightgown with small purple rosebuds that I had sewed for myself when my first child was born. It kept me warm during the night when I had to get up and feed the baby.

Colton and Amando's bedroom was right next to mine, and it was easy for me to hear them if they needed me during the night. I quietly opened my door so as not to wake Mateo and tiptoed across the hall. I gently opened the boys' door and peered into the dimly lit room. I had placed a night light in the room for these very occasions. Colton slept on the bottom bunk because he was the youngest and had just started sleeping in the room with his older brother. Previously, Alana and Amando shared a room until Colton's second birthday.

I walked into the bedroom and sat on the lower edge of Colton's bed where the guardrail wasn't present and whispered, "What's wrong, Colty?"

He said in between sobs, "Mommy, mouth hurts." I realized that he meant his gums. Having raised two older children, I knew Colton must be teething.

I reached my arms out to him and said, "Come here Colty. Let's get you something to make you feel better."

I carried his little body with his blue fleece footy pajamas into the kitchen. I sat him on a wooden chair while I got the medicine that has been used for centuries by all my Irish ancestors—whiskey. I poured some in a shot glass and set it on the kitchen table. I picked Colton up and set him on my lap. I dipped my index finger into the whiskey and said to my son, "This will make it better, Colty." I proceeded to massage the whiskey into his swollen gums without any protest from him.

When I finished rubbing his gums, I carried him over to the living room where my old maple rocking chair sat and began rocking Colton to sleep. I had put many miles on that rocking chair. I sang songs to my children when they were fussy or while I was nursing them in that wonderful chair.

One of their favorite songs that I sang was "Silent Night." After about fifteen minutes or so, Colton was fast asleep in my arms. I looked down at his beautiful angelic face, with his fair skin sprinkled with freckles and his golden-brown curls; my heart was full of love. I very carefully carried Colton down the hallway to his room and placed him gently down on his bed. I covered him with his blankets and kissed him on his soft cheek and whispered, "Goodnight my little Colty-boy. I love you."

I sleepily shuffled back to my room where I heard the quiet snores of my husband, fast asleep in the bed. I just shook my head and looked at the red digital numbers of the alarm clock reading 2:56 a.m. "Oh boy, I hope I get back to sleep," I said out loud.

That morning, I awoke with a start. The room was full of daylight. It was Sunday morning and a little after 8:00 a.m., which was late for me to wake up. I heard Colton talking to his brother in their room and smiled sleepily. I lay in bed, enjoying the warmth of my blankets. I heard Colton's little feet trotting down the hall to the family room to play with his toys. Then suddenly, I sat upright realizing that I had left the whiskey on the table last night. I jumped out of bed, threw open the door, and ran down the hallway. Mateo was yelling, "Mary, what the heck is wrong?" He was completely clueless about the events during the night.

I was about to turn the corner into the kitchen when I heard Colty making the sound of "Ahhhh . . ."

Then I heard the shot glass slam down on the oak table. As I came around the corner, I saw the glass being released by Colton's small, dimpled hand. I said, "Colty, what did you do? Drink the medicine?"

He said, "Yes, Mommy, good." He then smiled at me with his cute face.

I was astonished and felt guilty for leaving the whiskey on the kitchen table, but then I began to laugh and couldn't stop. Colton started giggling, too, and I picked him up and hugged him. I was quite aware that my son may have a penchant for alcohol, and I was going to have to keep an eye on him in the future.

Try to Love Again

I n 1994 I found out Mateo was seeing someone else. He had been emotionally distant and working a lot. Our relationship had become very strained, and he was becoming demanding about how I conducted the household. Our children were ages two, five, and seven. We had been married for nine years.

Then one night he said, "Mary, I am going out with a friend."

"Who?" I asked.

"Oh, you don't know him," he said casually.

"Where'd you meet him," I asked with curiosity.

"I met him at a meeting."

I could tell he was lying. After he left our home, it finally hit me. He wasn't having an affair with a woman, it was this guy. I put the kids to bed and went into my bedroom and sobbed. I was wide awake when he came home at 1:00 a.m., but I pretended to be asleep.

As soon as he got into bed and I heard his first snore, I quietly slipped off the mattress and went into the family room. I cried the entire night. I knew my life was forever changed. This man who I loved with all my heart had shattered mine, like a windshield in a head-on collision. I felt as though I had been in a car crash. Every bone and muscle in my body ached, and my brain felt jumbled. In the wee hours of the morning, I mentally divorced my husband.

My mind spun out of control. *What am I going to do? How can I go on living without him? What will I say to my children? When should I confront him about the situation?* I asked myself so many questions, like flashcards flipping through my brain. I decided to wait a couple of days until I calmed down before I mentioned the situation to him. It was going to take guts, but I had to talk to him. My life and the lives of my children depended on it.

Summer was quickly approaching; the end of school was in a couple of days. Alana and Amando were in second grade and kindergarten, respectively. I had committed to end-of-the-year activities at the elementary school where my kids attended. I volunteered as a music teacher, and I was singing with many of the students.

It was a Wednesday night and I had put the kids to bed. Mateo brushed his teeth and walked out of the bathroom into the bedroom. I took a deep breath and with a shaky voice asked him, "Who is that guy you went out with? Tell me the truth." I looked him straight in the eye. "Who is he?"

He cast his eyes down. He couldn't look at me, his shame apparent. He sat on the edge of the bed and started crying. "I am so sorry, Mary.

I had been a devoted and loyal wife, and I certainly did not deserve what was happening to me. He said, "Mary, if you really love me you won't leave me."

"So, you are telling me that you want me to

stay married to you while you go out and with men? I love myself much more than that. I deserve to be loved completely by another human being," I said with conviction.

I called Kaiser the next morning and asked to see a psychologist. I knew I needed help to deal with my situation. I also made an appointment with a nurse practitioner to get tested for HIV and a panel of STDs. I needed to make sure he had not passed a disease on to me or my children. When the results all came back negative, I thanked God.

I was able to express my anger, fear, and sadness to the counselor. The sessions helped me vent all the emotions I was going through. Mateo didn't want me to tell anyone about him being gay. I complied for two months until I set a plan in motion to get him to leave our home. I didn't tell my parents for those long two months. I grieved by myself at night after I put the kids to bed. Mateo was a firefighter, so he was gone every other night, which was quite helpful to me at the end of our marriage.

I signed up Alana and Amando for summer school. I walked Colton in a stroller around Lake Elizabeth, for miles and miles, until it was time to pick up Alana and Amando from school. I barely ate food, only enough to keep me alive. I lost twenty pounds in two months.

In early August, Aunt Jane was visiting my parents, and I knew having her around would give me the strength to tell my parents about my divorce. I invited her over to spend the night and told her first. I got a babysitter and drove my aunt to my mom and dad's house and told them everything. It was one of the most difficult talks I ever had with my parents, but I felt much better after I told them the truth. We all cried together. Dad was so understanding. It was the strongest connection that I ever felt with my father, and I was grateful to him for his support and love.

With much pushing and nagging, I was able to get Mateo to leave the house in September. I felt so free when he moved out of the house. I could breathe again. I was still hurt and angry, but it began to dissipate. I swore to myself that I would never marry again. I didn't think I could ever trust another man with my heart and soul.

I eventually dated several guys who were a few years younger than me, who had never been married and had no children. I had fun for a while, but soon realized they didn't understand me at all. They had no life experience or under-standing about what I had been through.

A year later, I met Duane. He was such a nice guy, kind and courteous. He treated me with respect. I went out with him a few times, and I knew that he really liked me. I told my counselor. I said, "I am going out with this guy named Duane. I really like him, but I know he wants to get serious, and I am scared. Is it too soon for me? Do I take a risk to open my heart again? What should I do?"

"Mary, you were alone in your marriage for

a long time. How do you feel when you are with Duane?"

"Great! We enjoy each other's company and he treats me well. He loves that I am a good mother and doesn't mind raising my three children. His friends think he is nuts for even going out with me." I laughed.

"Mary, you seem very happy. I have been counseling you for a year now, and I think your mind and heart are in the right place. I don't need to see you again. Go have a wonderful life."

A Weekend of My Own

I was going through a divorce. My children were ages 7, 5, and 3. It was a very stressful time. I tried to cope with the situation the best I could.

As the months went by, Mateo, my soon to be ex-husband, and I worked out a visitation schedule, which was a challenge because he was a firefighter. His days off varied, but I wasn't working, so I could be flexible. President's weekend in February was coming up, and Mateo told me he was going to have the kids during that time. I agreed. *What am I going to do?* I decided to go away for the weekend alone. I had never done that before. I was a little nervous, but gosh darn it, I was going to do it! "Where should I go?" I said out loud. I gave it some thought and decided to go to Pacific Grove. It was one of my favorite places, and it wasn't too long a drive, so I called and made a reservation at The Oak Motel.

When the weekend arrived, I was very excited. I dropped the kids off with their dad and kissed them all goodbye. It was strange to go on a trip by myself. I had married at twenty-two and had my first child by twenty-four and had always gone places with my family, never alone. I was ready to be an independent woman.

I packed a small bag and loaded my royal blue 10-speed bike in the back of the van. I put in my favorite CD and off I went. What an adventure. I wasn't going to have to take care of anyone but myself. It was a beautiful warm clear day in mid-February. I got onto the I-680 freeway heading south from Washington Avenue in Fremont. When I arrived in San Jose, I took the101 freeway south to Prunedale and Highway 68 to the coast toward Monterey.

I reached Pacific Grove in an hour and a half. No fussy kids, no having to stop for potty breaks, no, "Are we there yet?" I was very familiar with Monterey and Pacific Grove because I had gone there as a child and many times as an adult. I learned to scuba dive in the icy cold waters of the Monterey Bay. I drove down Lighthouse Avenue from Monterey to Pacific Grove, looking for the address of my motel. It was just off the main drag near the Point Pinos Lighthouse.

I checked in, and the older woman in the office asked, "Will there be anyone else checking in with you?"

I said, "No, just me." It was so foreign to me, being alone. I felt light. I got the key and walked to my room and opened the door. I placed my bag on the dresser and then headed out the door. It was a great day to ride my bike. I unlocked the back hatch of the van and pulled out my bike. I had removed the plastic baby seat before I left Fremont. I wanted to feel free and not have any reminders of having children lest I have moments of missing them.

I rode my bike down to Ocean Drive, which

snaked its way along the coast. The briny wind blew through my long strawberry blonde hair and I felt light, like a feather being blown about in the air. What a fantastic experience. It was just what my body and soul needed. As I rode along the shore, I saw numerous sea birds: pelicans, gulls, sandpipers, and cormorants. The waves rolled in, crashing on the jagged rocks and splashing a fine mist in the air. Many people were walking, driving, or riding their bikes and enjoying the rare winter sunshine.

I stopped at a Thai restaurant and ordered Pad Thai, one of my favorite dishes, and ate while I watched the people and the scenery. I then went to a shop nearby and bought a beautiful backpack. The material was a colorful Southwest pattern of red, orange, blue, and gold. I put it on and off I rode.

It was becoming dusk and I headed back to my hotel when I heard a high-pitched squeaking, *What could that be?* I came around a corner near the lighthouse, and there before my eyes was a man, formally dressed in a Scottish kilt, playing the bagpipes. I pulled off the road and parked my bike. I sat on a rock about twenty feet from the Scotsman, mesmerized by the bagpipes. What a sensational treat it was for me to watch a colorful sunset over the Pacific coupled with the soulful sounds being played on the pipes. What a special end to a lovely day of my weekend on my own.

Jill, Amando, Colton, and Alana

Jill, we first met on your dad's and my second
date.
You offered me Jelly Bellies, a smile on your
face.
Your father spoke of marriage, couldn't wait,
But we needed to find the right time and place.
You and my three kids got along well,
Playing around, swimming in the pool.
We decided where we would dwell,
Wanted you to go to a good school.
He and I married at your Papa's house.
I sewed a white brocade and green velvet dress
for you.
During the ceremony, you were as quiet as a
mouse.
I gave you a gold locket to show my
commitment was true.
It has been twenty-five years since that special
day.
The passage of time blows me away.

Wedding Day

Mary and Duane

Bride gazes at her groom with smiling eyes,
He looks into the camera, flashes a grin.
You can hear friends' and family's sighs,
Commemorating the couple's life to begin.
Husband makes a champagne toast,
Wife chimes in too.
He is modest, won't boast
About the new wife, he did woo.
What will their new life bring?
Many years together?
Cherished offspring?
Hardships to weather?
Twenty-four years after their wedding day,
The wise couple has learned to play and pray.

Duane, Mary, Jill, Alana, Colton, and Amando

"Mommy, What's Barf?"

Colton at six

While my children were growing up, I always encouraged conversation during dinnertime. Each night, while we ate our food, I asked each of my five kids what happened at school that day, which often led to some colorful explanations.

One night, Colton, a kindergartener at the time, asked me an interesting question. "Mommy, what's barf?"

I gazed into my son's big blue eyes, wondering why he was asking me this question. His innocent freckled face looked up at me, patiently waiting for an answer.

After a few seconds, I finally answered him. "Colty, barf is another word for vomit. You know, the stuff that comes out of your mouth when you throw up. Why do you ask?"

My son looked puzzled, his face scrunched

in a frown, and then he said, "Mommy, today at school my teacher read me a story about how deers eat barf off trees. Why would deers do that?"

I tried not to laugh. "Colty, I am pretty sure your teacher said that deer eat bark off trees, not barf. Bar-f and bar-k do sound a lot alike," I said, annunciating each consonant loudly. "Can you hear the difference, Colty?"

By this time, my husband and our other children were laughing uncontrollably, and finally, Colty and I joined in too.

Valentine

I n 1997 I went to visit my parents on Valentine's Day and happily brought them chocolates and flowers. I was five months pregnant with my fourth child and lived only a mile away, which was good because they were elderly. I was glad I had moved back home to Livermore two years previously. They were going to be celebrating their forty-eighth wedding anniversary in less than a month. I was hoping with all my heart they would make it to their fiftieth.

My parents met at a Naval Officer's Club in Philadelphia, back in 1948. My father was twenty-nine years old and had been in the Navy for ten years and had endured World War II as a prisoner of war for three and a half years. My mother was twenty-one years old and had just joined the Navy as a newly capped nurse from New York City.

My father told me that when he first laid eyes on my mother, a brunette beauty, he was instantly smitten. On the other hand, my mother told me that she noticed how handsome my dad was, but he was quiet and shy. She was eyeing one of the Canadian officers who had been talking with my father.

Well, as the story goes, my father asked her to dance and he was a great dancer and swept my mom off her feet. By the end of the evening, they were in the back seat of a convertible riding down the main drag in Philly, kissing while another officer drove. Six months later they were married.

I always loved hearing my mom and dad tell their how-we-met story. It made me feel so cheerful and romantic. I had observed over the years the deep love and connection between my parents, and I prayed that I would have the same connection with my husband after so many years.

After I heard my parent's story for the one-hundredth time, I noticed a beautiful Valentine card sitting on the bar area where they always sat together in the evenings where they drank their highballs and caught up on happenings. It was the most gorgeous Valentine I had ever seen. It was trimmed with lace and gilded with gold ink, a card that needed extra postage because it was so large. I commented on its beauty to my father and how lucky my mother was to receive such a lovely Valentine. Then I opened the card. I don't remember what words were printed inside, only the one word my father had written in all capital letters: Forever.

It was the last card my father gave my mother because he died four months later. I will never forget that day, and how I cried as I read that one significant word my father wrote to his one and only Valentine.

Goodbye, Love

I woke up with a start as my unborn child danced the rumba in my belly. The day was May 30, 1997. My due date was in two weeks, but I was more than ready to have this baby because as a few thoughtless people said, "You're as big as a house." I had given birth to my oldest son, Amando eight years before, and he weighed in at ten pounds, eleven ounces. Colton had weighed eight pounds, eleven ounces. I had a feeling this baby was going to be the same as Amando.

As I lay in bed, remembering what I had to do this day, I grew forlorn. The health of my father was declining so Colleen and I were going to take him to the Veteran's Hospital in Livermore to be admitted. Our mother was not able to care for our father anymore because she had become blind from macular degeneration and frail from osteoporosis.

Carefully rolling on my side, I threw my legs over the edge of the bed, placed my feet firmly on the floor, and pushed myself off the mattress. After coming to a standing position, I gazed out the window and noticed the beautiful clear spring day. A news reporter on TV the previous night claimed today would be warm. I waddled to my closet looking for a dress to wear and took out a navy shift with magenta flowers. In my advanced pregnancy, my body had become prone to overheating.

My husband, Duane, had already left for work. Jill was in eighth grade at Mendenhall Middle School. I knew she was awake because I heard her music playing in her room next to mine, I walked into my sons' room, singing to them, "Rise and shine and give God your glory, glory." They opened their sleepy eyes, smiling. I watched them stir then left their room to walk downstairs to Alana's room to make sure she was also awake. I carefully stepped down each stair holding the oak banister. As I entered the family room, I heard the sound of the shower running in the bathroom. Knowing that Alana had gotten up, I walked into the kitchen to start making their lunches. Peanut butter and jelly was the usual bill of fare. Grabbing supplies from the pantry, I began assembling the sandwiches.

Mindlessly spreading peanut butter on slices of Wonder bread, I thought of the radical changes that were going to take place when my father left his home. Tears welled in my eyes, and I tried to hold them back when I heard the boys hopping down the stairs. No use getting the kids upset before school, I thought, drying my eyes.

The girls entered the kitchen, and the four of them sat eating cereal, happily chatting together. Once they finished eating, I sent them off to brush their teeth. Finally, I called them out to our minivan to drive them to school.

I first drove Jill to her school, and dropped

her off, saying goodbye. Then we headed to Rancho Las Positas Elementary School where my three youngest attended, and where I was also the music teacher. I parked in the school lot, grabbed my guitar, and walked my three children to the playground where I said goodbye to them.

Playing my guitar and singing with the students would be a wonderful distraction from what I knew I had to do later in the day. I loved being a music teacher because the children were always happy to see me. I was like a favorite aunt bringing presents.

At 11:45 a.m., I finished my fifth music class for the day, packed up my guitar, and drove to my parent's house on Sunset Drive, less than a mile away.

I met Colleen in front of the house where we grew up. I gave her a long hug. Everyone in the family knew what was going to happen today because we had all conferred with each other by phone. Even our mother, with much hesitation, had agreed to the plan. Life with my father was becoming too difficult for her. Even though she didn't want him to leave their home, she knew her husband's health was failing, and she couldn't help him anymore.

Colleen and I entered the house. I said, "Hello Mom, it's us."

"Oh, you're here," her voice faint. Dad was sitting in his worn La-Z-Boy recliner.

"Hi, Dad. How are you doing today?" Colleen said gently.

"Not so good, Coll."

"Well, Dad, we know. Mary and I are going to take you to the VA Hospital today. We need to get you checked out. Okay?" she said softly.

"Okay, girls. I am getting too much for your mother. Let's get going."

Dad rose weakly out of his chair. Mom was sitting on the couch very quiet. I was still standing in the living room trying to stay calm. I lumbered to the front door, opened the screen door, reached up and moved the metal bracket to keep it open, and walked onto the front porch. The overhang kept it cool on warm days. Colleen came out and stood on the stoop and watched while my mom and dad said goodbye to each other. They hugged and tenderly kissed. My father was seventy-seven years old, my mom sixty-nine.

By this time, Colleen and I were openly crying, trying not to sob. I was witnessing the most intimate scene of my life. My mother and father said goodbye to each other after forty-eight years of marriage, knowing my dad was never going to return to their home or the bed they shared for so many years.

We didn't want to separate them, but we had no choice, and our parents both knew it. They held each other for a while longer, and then my dad said. "Goodbye, love." Colleen helped our father down the step and led him to her car.

I walked over to my mom and gave her a big hug and said, "Mom, we will take good care of

Dad. We'll call you when we get Dad settled." I left her and she shut the door slowly. I followed Colleen in my car to the VA hospital, five miles away.

After assessing my father, the doctor at the VA ordered an ambulance to take him to Valley Care Hospital; he was in respiratory arrest. They didn't have the emergency equipment needed for our dad's care at the VA.

Upon his arrival, they hooked my dad up to a breathing machine, and I never heard my father's voice again.

My Father's Eyes

Pat, Colleen, Peg, Chris (in uniform), Mark, Katy, and Mary,
Presidio Cemetery 1997

T he ventilator made strange sucking noises, but it kept my father alive with the much-needed oxygen that his lungs craved. His two-pack-a-day habit for the last sixty years had finally caught up with him. Ironically, he did not have lung cancer, but emphysema. *Dad used to look commanding to me when I was a kid, and now his body is so fragile.* I looked helplessly at him in the cold metal hospital bed.

Tonight, the ventilator would be taken away. Dad had been on the machine for a week. My mother had gone against his wishes by allowing the medical personnel to hook him up to the breathing machine so family members could fly in from various parts of the country to say goodbye. She, herself, was not ready to let him go. He had been on a ventilator two other times in the last several years when he had pneumonia. I heard him tell my mother one day, "I hate that godawful machine, love. If I end up in the hospital again, I don't want it."

I sat in an uncomfortable plastic chair at Valley Care Medical Center in Pleasanton, California. My nine-month pregnant belly rested on my thighs. I gazed at Dad's heart monitor, listening to the blips of his heartbeat. I pivoted toward the blood pressure machine when I heard it automatically take his pressure and the cuff crackled as it filled with air. Hospitals tend to have a specific smell, disinfectant, and fear. I believe the collective energy of the people visiting their loved ones causes anxiety to permeate the air.

Aunt Jane stood near the hospital bed, holding my father's hand and stroking his snowy, baby-fine hair. Gosh, I loved my Dad's hair. I enjoyed touching it. I always ask his permission first, and he chuckled and said, "Ah, go ahead, Mimi." I especially liked to feel his hair right after he took a shower and hadn't put any Brylcreem in it.

Aunt Jane was so gentle with my father. She adored him. She first met him when she was seven. You see, my mother was fourteen years older than her sister, Jane. Mom met Dad when she was twenty-one and a nurse at an officer's club in Philadelphia. When Mom brought him home to meet her family, Aunt Jane told me how handsome he looked in his Naval uniform. He made quite an impression on my aunt, and she had admired him ever since.

Today would be one of the hardest days of my life. I had to say goodbye to my father. The doctor had told us that once the ventilator was removed, Dad would probably die in less than twenty-four hours.

Aunt Jane said, "Dick, I want to call a priest to give you your last rites. Is that okay with you?"

Dad couldn't talk with the tube going down his throat, but he nodded his head. My eyes filled with tears. My dad converted to Catholicism to marry my mother. Now, that's what I call true love. He hadn't been to church since I was ten years old. He and my mom stopped attending, and I never knew why, but Dad and God had a personal relationship. I had always known that God had saved Dad's life time and time again during his time in the Japanese prison camp. Dad had told me the brutal stories while I was growing up.

Aunt Jane left the room to make the call. I struggled to get out of the hard chair and went to my dad's bedside. It was my turn to take his hand and stroke his hair. "Dad, this is so difficult, saying goodbye to you. Thank you for giving me life and for taking care of me. I promise to take good care of Mom. You don't need to worry about that. I know how it concerns you. I love you so much. Thanks for being there for me when I was getting a divorce. You were my rock. Hey, Dad, I am pretty sure I am going to have a baby boy. I spoke with Duane and if we do have a son, we want his middle name to be Richard after you. I am so sorry that you aren't going to meet my son. I wish you could hold on longer, but it's time for you to go. It's okay to let go, Dad. I am going to miss you so much." My father's eyes showed me so much love.

Aunt Jane returned to the room. "The priest will be here in fifteen minutes. Mimi, go get something to drink and go to the restroom now. I want you to be here for your Dad's last rites."

I squeezed Dad's hand, kissed his forehead, and walked slowly out of the room, wiping tears off my cheeks. I looked at my aunt and she was crying too. Our eyes met and we gave each other a look of compassion.

I took my break and returned ten minutes later. I sat on the chair quietly until the priest arrived. I can't remember his name, but I was grateful he came. He stood by the bed and prayed for my father. Aunt Jane and I were near the foot of the bed, bearing witness to my father's last rites. The priest anointed my father with holy oil and blessed him. My father nodded when he was asked to be forgiven for his sins. My father's clear blue eyes understood every word spoken to him. It was an honor to be there during such a simple, yet sacred ritual.

When the priest finished, we thanked him,

and my aunt walked with him out of the room. I stood next to my father. "Dad, you can let go whenever you are ready. You have been blessed and God is waiting for you. I will see you again one day. I love you, Dad."

It was extremely difficult for me to leave the hospital that afternoon, but I had a husband and four children at home who needed me too.

That evening, they removed the tube from my father's throat, unplugged the machine, and wheeled it away. I received a call from my aunt the next morning telling me my dad had passed away during the night. She said she didn't want to wake me because I needed my rest. My brother, Mark, had been with our dad when he passed. I was so glad that my father didn't die alone. I was thankful that I had said a proper goodbye and witness him preparing to meet his Father. My father died on June 6, D-Day, so poignant, since he was a veteran of WWII. Thirteen days later, I gave birth to a nine-pound son and named him Samuel Richard Duane Heaton. And so the wonderful circle of life begins again.

Dad at twenty-nine

Parents came from Denmark by steamer ship.
The youngest child of five to an aged father.
Would never dream of giving Papa any lip.
No time for the littlest, they didn't bother.
Spent hours along the Columbia River, fishing
for salmon, eating wild blueberries.
Coming out of the cold water made him shiver.
Enjoyed country living, he had no worries.
His eldest sister loved him dearly.
When Papa died, he moved to her ranch.
There he could see life much more clearly.
Wanted to join the military, which branch?
Served his country, was a prisoner of war.
The memories of the carnage he bore.

Livermore Saloon

Back when the new millennium was approaching and Sam was two years old, I came to the realization I needed to make some changes in my life. I craved an outlet where I could socialize with adults but feel young again. Being a good girl had taken its toll on me, and I needed some fun and relaxation.

I came up with a good idea to start up a co-ed softball team. Duane already played on a men's team, on Wednesday nights, so I thought, Why don't we play on a team together on Friday nights? Our two daughters were the perfect babysitting age, sixteen and twelve. They were available most Friday nights to watch their three little brothers, ages ten, eight, and two.

I had always enjoyed playing baseball with my brothers when I was a kid. I wanted to play softball in high school but I got a job at fourteen, and it took up most of my free time. Playing ball got pushed aside. So at the age of thirty-seven, I started playing softball. I played second base, and I tried my best to field the ball if it was hit in my direction, but many times it whizzed by me. I could hit the ball well and eventually my fielding skills improved.

I enjoyed getting to know my teammates, who were mainly married couples. We began to go out after the games to a bar downtown called the Livermore Saloon. It was located east of the flagpole on First Street where the Beer Baron is currently located.

It was a wonderful old space, dark, long, and narrow. I'm sure the decor had not changed much over the last hundred years. The bar was about thirty feet long and made of polished wood. Behind the bar was a counter and shelves, which held a multitude of colorful bottles of liquor. Behind the bottles, a mirror on the wall reflected the bright hues into my eyes. I took pleasure in looking at the various shapes of bottles: tall, skinny, heart-shaped, triangular, and cylindrical. Some were even made of ceramic clay and hand-painted.

My favorite detail of the saloon was the shelf that encircled the entire room ten feet from the ground. On it were at least fifty different kinds of Martini shakers. Many were antiques made with ruby and cobalt glass with chrome trim. I sipped my Sierra Nevada beer while I gazed at the stunning shaker collection.

I appreciated the saloon's decor, but my favorite part of coming to the bar was the karaoke. I always loved to sing as a kid, and I sang in the high school choir, but singing at the saloon was thrilling. The guy that ran the karaoke machine was named Abe. He was a tall, thin man with gray hair and a mustache. He appeared to be in his late sixties and wore a baseball cap to cover his balding head. He also happened to own the Livermore Saloon.

Abe's karaoke machine was set up at the far end of the bar, opposite the front door. He had placed a microphone on a stand and a monitor to the left of it so the words of the song displayed as the music played. He had several black binders with lists of hundreds of songs to choose from. I remember the first time I signed up to sing, I was so nervous. I chose "Your Song" by Elton John because I knew it by heart.

As I sat and waited for my name to be called, my heart beat rapidly and my palms sweated. I felt my face turn red. I was grateful that the bar was dimly lit, and the patrons couldn't see how flushed my skin was. When Abe called my name, I walked slowly down the narrow room, and my pulse quickened with each step. He handed me the microphone and smiled. As I stood looking at my teammates and other people sitting at the bar as well as the patrons sitting at the little tables along the opposite wall, I thought, Why the heck did I want to sing in front of all these people?

I heard the introduction to the song and my mind went blank. I quickly looked at the screen where the words began to appear, opened my mouth, and began to sing. It was strange to hear a voice coming out of the speakers above me. *Was that really my voice? I didn't sound half bad.*

After the first verse, I relaxed a bit and the song rematerialized in my brain. I looked out at the people in the saloon, and they smiled at me. Wow, what a great feeling to sing in front of people. The song ended and I handed the microphone back to Abe. He said, "Mary, great job. Make sure you come back again."

After my first experience with karaoke, I was hooked. Every Friday after our softball game, Duane and I went to the Livermore Saloon. Many times, we stayed until closing so I could sing one more song. If I was lucky, I got to sing four times a night, but other times if the bar was extremely crowded, I only got a turn twice.

Playing softball and singing karaoke became my new outlets. I had been a mother for twelve years, not getting out much and socializing with people, so in coming to the saloon, I could relax. I hadn't worked much in those twelve years and felt a bit isolated at times. Mainly, it was the sense of responsibility that got to me. At the Livermore Saloon, I drank a couple of beers and I didn't have to be on alert watching my kids. I hadn't drunk much alcohol in the past because I was either pregnant or breastfeeding my children. I didn't even party in high school or college. I had my first baby at the age of twenty-four. I kind of missed out on being a teenager, always choosing to be responsible and practical.

I loved showing up at the bar and have the bartender call me by name. I also made friends with other karaoke singers. We regulars had envelopes with our names on them, filled with little slips of white paper with the numbers and titles of our favorite songs. Coming to the saloon made me feel young and free. I could leave my responsibilities back home and let loose.

One night, a year after we had been going to the saloon, Duane was acting peculiar. I heard

Abe call the name Alan. Suddenly, Duane began walking up to Abe and grabbed the microphone. Duane dedicated the song to me. I was in shock. I couldn't believe my shy husband was going to perform in front of a crowd of people. He started to sing "Love's Got a Hold" by Alan Jackson. I was so touched and proud of him singing the song.

It was more fun having Duane sing karaoke too. We had a good run at the saloon. It lasted about five years until Abe sold the bar to a guy named Sid. One evening, Sid said to Duane and me, "I wanna draw a younger crowd into this bar." And he did.

Well, we knew that Sid was hinting to us that we were too old, so we never went back. We heard that Abe was doing karaoke at Granada Bowl and we sang there several times, but it just wasn't the same. I missed the comfy atmosphere of the Livermore Saloon, a favorite haunt I shall always remember with a smile on my face and a song in my heart.

Peggy at twenty-two

P eggy was the second child born out of seven. She was eleven years older than I, and I loved her dearly. When I was young, she was the sibling who dyed Easter eggs with me and put my makeup on for Halloween. Unfortunately, Peggy got married when I was nine years old and moved to Clovis, New Mexico, with her husband, Dan who had just joined the Air Force.

I wrote letters to my sister and sometimes she'd write back. I missed her terribly. A year went by and we got a call that she and Dan were moving to Wiesbaden, Germany. I was devastated because I wouldn't see her again until I was thirteen.

When she came home from Germany, they rented a bungalow on College Avenue. I was so happy, but after six months she came over to tell us they were moving to Auburn.

Peggy drove her VW Bug to Livermore for a visit and she took Chris, Mark, and me back with her to Auburn. She drove us to the American River several miles from her house, and we swam together. We all had a blast.

I adored Peggy's "little house on the prairie," as my mom used to call it. I loved the claw-foot bathtub and the old pedestal sink in the bathroom. The stove in the kitchen was from the 40s, and a wood-burning stove was the only source of heat in her house.

Peggy's husband left her one winter's day without saying goodbye. She saw him with their truck loaded up with their stuff, driving the opposite direction from her on highway 49. She found out later that he was having an affair with their former real estate agent. It was a blow to Peggy, but no one in our family ever liked the guy.

In six months, Peggy went to see her doctor because she had been experiencing dizzy spells and double vision. He performed a few simple neurological tests in his office and immediately made an appointment for Peggy to see Dr. Maas, a neurosurgeon in Sacramento, in two days.

After the CT scan was taken, Dr. Maas informed Peggy she had a baseball-size tumor in the back of her skull, and it needed to be taken out as soon as possible. She called my parents to inform them of her predicament. Our family was in shock.

We drove up to see my sister before her surgery. I remember going into the pre-op area while a nurse shaved off Peggy's long, dark brown hair. I remember hugging her tightly, with tears running down my cheeks, wondering if I would ever see her again. I said, "Peg, I'll see you in a few hours. I love you so much." I couldn't and wouldn't say goodbye to her.

Mom, Dad, and I sat in the tiny waiting room. Aunt Jane flew in from New York City, where she was a nursing instructor at St. Vincent's Hospital. We had been waiting four hours by the time she arrived. Three more hours dragged by until Dr. Maas came out of the ER looking fatigued. He said, "Well, Peggy's in stable condition. The tumor was benign and the size of my fist. I was able to get most of it out. But I had to leave a little piece because each time I tried to extract it; she would stop breathing. I decided to leave it alone. It may grow back one day."

My father shook Dr. Maas's hand and thanked him. We all were crying with relief as we saw the orderlies wheeling Peggy out of the OR to the recovery room down the hall. She had all sorts of tubes and wires connected to her, but she was alive.

After a week, Peggy was able to come home because Aunt Jane was going to care for her. Peggy could not walk, talk, or dress in the beginning. She had to learn how to do all those things over again. Slowly, with time and physical therapy she was receiving from Aunt Jane, she recovered. Peggy's gross and fine motor skills were never completely the same. She eventually moved back to Auburn.

After about a year, Peggy sold her house and came to live with my parents because she lost confidence in herself. She didn't have the speed to do her work, and her speech was slightly affected. After a few years, she moved into an apartment on "I" Street in Livermore. She became a teller for US Bank and worked there for many years. She had a good life, and I visited her often. We became best friends and she loved to see my kids because she never had any of her own. She never married again.

In December of 1995, Peggy had to have another surgery. A cyst had formed in the middle of her brain. That operation went well, and she recovered quickly. But in 2000 after her annual CT scan, her neurosurgeon, Dr. Taghioff, informed her the tumor had grown back and was the size of a golf ball. Peggy told me she didn't want to go through another surgery, but she eventually consented.

On February 6, 2000, Colleen, Katy, and I sat in the Valley Care Hospital waiting area while Peggy had her third brain surgery. Once again, we didn't know if Peggy was going to survive the operation. When Dr. Taghioff came out of the OR with a smile on his face we knew that Peggy was alive.

Peggy's recovery was slow, and she stayed in the San Ramon Rehabilitation Hospital for a month. She had speech, physical, and occupational therapy every day. When she left the hospital, she stayed at Katy's house. Peggy had been living there for two months when her head began to swell. Dr. Taghioff told her too much spinal fluid was collecting in her skull, and he needed to put a shunt in to let it flow down to her spinal cord. He did the procedure on June 2nd. It went well and Chris was there to greet her after the quick surgery. She felt fine, so he went home in the afternoon. I called her that evening and she said, "Mary I haven't felt this good in years." I was so happy for her.

At three o'clock in the morning, the phone rang, and I answered it. Colleen called to tell me Peggy had died. I fell to my knees sobbing. *How could this happen?* Peggy told me she felt great. *How was I going to live without her?* Duane drove us to the hospital early that morning because none of us could believe she was gone, we had to see for ourselves. When we entered the room, I knew Peggy's spirit had left this world. The body lying on the bed was only a shell.

A week later, I held Peggy's memorial service at my house. I sang "Angel" by Sarah McLaughlin for my sister. My entire family was devastated by the loss of Peggy.

Two weeks after Peggy died, she came to me in my sleep. I was sitting on a step at our parent's house sobbing because I missed her so much. She sat next to me and hugged me and said, "Mary, don't be sad. I am so happy now. I am where I want to be. Please don't cry for me anymore." She smiled radiantly. I woke up from the dream and felt Peggy's spirit envelop me. A sense of peace washed over my body. I felt comforted by her presence and words. I knew that she was finally at peace and I smiled. I knew it was time for me to move forward with my life.

The Oak Tree

The oak tree has been waiting patiently for me for almost 400 years. It stands guarding our family cabin in a little town called Greeley Hill near Yosemite. It watches over our mountain home until we arrive one weekend a month.

The tree is a majestic white oak about seventy feet tall. My hugging arms cannot encircle the thick mossy trunk. Its hundreds of branches reach up to the sky trying to capture the sun's glorious warmth. It is old and gnarled, with patches of moss and lichen. It stands near the deck of the cabin.

When I visit the cabin, the first thing I do is to go outside and sit in a chair on the deck and gaze upon the tree's regal beauty. I can see its many branches, almost feeling as if I am sitting in it. I wonder what the tree has seen in its 400 years of life. How many people have walked beneath it? How many animals have lived in it?

Four hundred years ago, the tree was a tiny sapling, just starting to grow. It was young and didn't have many leaves. I imagine a Miwok family walking beside it, not noticing the little tree as they stop for the night on their trek to Yosemite Valley. They spend their summers there and enjoy gazing upon Tissiack, the half dome. The miniature tree sees its first humans and hears them talk in quiet voices.

Two hundred and fifty years go by and the tree has become big and strong. Its branches radiate out from a formidable trunk. It has seen many people of the Miwok tribe who have been grateful for its shade from the hot summer sun. They had respect for the tree.

A hundred years go by and the tree hears a different voice, much louder and crass. The oak hears a man and his donkey walking by it. The man's tools and pans are strapped to the animal. They clank loudly as he walks by the tree. He is a miner on his way to find gold in the nearby Merced River.

During the oak's life, it has seen thousands of deer, bear, squirrels, birds, and millions of insects, which makes the tree happy.

Then one day thirty-five years ago, a man named Al bought the land where the tree lives. Al loved the tree and wanted to build his home next to it. He built it with care and decided to name the road that led to his house, Lone Oak Drive. He watched the tree change with the seasons, admiring its beauty.

Al was getting older and decided to sell his house. Many people came to see it, but no one bought it. Nearly two years went by until Duane saw the house for sale on the Internet. We decided to take a drive to look at the house, which was a two and a half-hour drive from Livermore.

When we arrived at the house and walked inside, we instantly fell in love with it. I walked onto the deck and saw the beautiful oak tree and said, "This tree has been waiting for me."

The tree and I became friends and have a mutual respect. I love to gaze upon it every day while I am at the cabin. I talk to it. I enjoy the cooling shade it creates each summer day. I love to gaze at it in the fall as the leaves let go and flutter to the ground. In the winter, the snow clings to its branches and clothes it in white crystals. In spring, I see the buds form on the branches and watch as they unfurl before my eyes.

The tree and I are connected. The oak tree is happy to have me as a friend. It will live much longer than I. When I die, the tree will keep watch over my children and grandchildren, which brings me much comfort.

New Roof

I n 2003, when we purchased our cabin in the mountains near Yosemite, it was obvious the roof was not going to last long. It was a cedar shake roof that was put on in 1980. We paid for an inspection, and the roof was certified for two more years. When we received the warranty from the roofing inspector, we breathed a collective sigh of relief.

Two plus years went by and we enjoyed visiting our cabin every month. On Memorial weekend 2005, I contently curled up on the couch reading a book when an icy drop hit my scalp. I gazed at the knotty pine boards above me and searched for the source of water. After a few minutes of staring at the ceiling, I went back to reading, and I was nailed by another drop.

Duane sat across from me on a loveseat upholstered in a Southwest fabric of red, blue, and beige. I dreaded giving him the unfortunate news, but there was no way I could keep my discovery quiet.

"Duane, honey, I hate to tell you this, but I just felt two drops of water on my head. I think we have a leak in the roof."

"What? Are you kidding me? Are you sure?" His face contorted with anger.

"Yes, Duane. I felt drops. The water's cold here."

"Darn it. I knew this roof wasn't going to

last. I don't know why the former owner put a shake roof in the first place. It's such a fire hazard."

During the next month, we contacted a few roofers. We drove to one in Sonora, and it seemed like a good company because they had been around for twenty-five years. They were even willing to drive to our cabin in Greeley Hill to do the work. The company wanted $12,000 for a new roof, which was a steep price for us. So we decided to ask for recommendations from our friends.

A few weeks later, I was visiting my friend, Liz and she said, "You know, Mary, last year we hired a guy named Trevor to put a roof on my in-law's cabin up in Arnold. He did a good job, and he didn't mind driving up there to do the work. You should give him a call. He will probably put on the roof for less money."

She gave me his phone number and I gave it to Duane. He called Trevor that night and we set up an appointment with him at our house to get an estimate. Trevor gave us a quote of $10,000, so we decided to go with him. We picked out thirty-year composition shingles, which were chocolate brown with small flecks of hunter green. We thought the natural colors would complement our mountain home and its surroundings.

We set up a weekend in early July for Trevor and his workers to drive up to the cabin. We let them stay at our place, so they could get the work done in one weekend and wouldn't have to go back and forth to the Bay Area. We kept in contact with him by landline and told him to call us if he had any questions.

Trevor and his crew arrived early Saturday morning with two large trucks loaded with shingles, tar paper, and plywood. The first part of the job was to remove the old cedar shingles. Then, plywood was nailed to the exposed roof slats, and tar paper stapled on top of the plywood. This process was going to take up most of the day and on Sunday, the new shingles would be nailed on the roof.

Duane called Saturday evening to check in with Trevor.

"Hey Trevor, how's it going? Were you able to get all the old shingles off and get the plywood and tar paper on today?"

"Yeah, Duane, we did, but it took us a lot longer than we thought."

"Oh, yeah? Why's that, Trevor?"

"Well, me and my two guys were up on the roof pulling off the old shingles when suddenly, bats started flying out at us. It was crazy. There must have been two hundred or more. I've never seen anything like it."

"Really? Wow, I've seen bats flying around at dusk, and knew there were some behind the gutters, but I didn't think they were under the shingles. Sorry about that, Trevor."

"Well, that's okay. We got the job done. We'll get the new shingles on tomorrow."

"Okay, Trevor. Thanks for all the hard work. I appreciate it."

We were eager to see our new roof but were not able to get up to our cabin for a few more weeks. When we finally arrived, we were very happy with our new roof. It took years off the look of our mountain home. And we certainly were glad to be rid of the hundreds of bats living under our shingles.

We enjoyed our stay at the cabin that weekend. On Sunday, we happened to run into some friends at the breakfast held at the community center. Jim and Dawn were well-known artists in town. We had recently purchased some of their work. We had also rented a cottage from them over two years ago when we began looking for a cabin in the area.

"Hi, Dawn and Jim. It's great to see you two. How's it going?"

Dawn gave us hugs and said, "Great to see you, Mary and Duane."

"So anything new since we saw you last? I asked.

"Well, yes. The strangest thing happened a few weeks ago. A colony of bats took up residence in the eaves of the community center. We have no idea where they came from. It was the darndest thing," Dawn said.

I tried to keep a straight face and said, "Really? Wow, I wonder where they came from."

I looked over at Duane and raised my left eyebrow and he had a slight smirk on his face. I had to look away from Duane. We continued to chat with Dawn and Jim for a few minutes and then excused ourselves.

"Well, it was great seeing you both. We are heading back to Livermore now. Take care. We'll be back in a few weeks."

We hugged them and headed to our van, got in, and plopped in our seats. We looked at each other and burst out laughing.

Once I caught my breath I said, "Oh my God, Duane, I could barely contain myself in front of Dawn and Jim."

"I know, Mary. Me too. Can you believe our bats ended up roosting at the community center? That's insane."

"Well, I'll never tell."

Sophie, the Clearance Dog

Sophie

ophie, our pet Weimaraner, is dark charcoal gray, what is called a blue Weimaraner, which is not recognized by the AKC. Most Weims are a silver or tawny color, but Sophie's coat is much darker. She glistens when the sun shines upon her and at night, she is invisible. She is about two inches shorter than the average female Weim because she was the runt of the litter and weighs 65 pounds instead of 75.

In 2003 my family purchased a cabin in the mountains an hour west of Yosemite in a little town called Greeley Hill. My five children had been pestering me for years to get a dog, but I was very resistant because I had enough mammals to take care of. I had my dog Clancy when the kids were babies, and I remember how much work it was. I felt guilty that I didn't get to spend enough quality time with Clancy because I gave most of my attention to my kids. I swore I wouldn't get another dog until I could be a good mother to it.

In September my family was at our cabin and the kids started asking me about getting a dog for the thousandth time. I told them I was finally getting to the point where I was ready to purchase a dog in December I said. My youngest child, Sam, was six years old at the time and in first grade. I thought that he was independent enough, and I had extra time on my hands since he was going to school from 8:30 a.m. to 2:30 p.m. every day. That night I went to sleep at the cabin, and I began to think about getting a dog. When I woke up in the morning, I found a local paper in our cabin called the *Yosemite Herald* and started looking in the want ads. I went to the Dogs and Cats section and started calling numbers. The paper was a month old and most of the dogs had been sold or given away. I came to the last ad which said, Weimaraners: $600. I called the phone number and spoke with Margaret, who was very kind. She told me she had one puppy left and that she was a runt. I said, "Then you must not want $600 for her?"

"I will only charge you $100 to cover the shots and tail docking fee from the vet," Margaret said.

"Will you please give me directions to your home? We will come to see the puppy in an hour."

It took us over an hour to get to Tuolumne

City where they lived. When we arrived at Margaret's house, several dogs greeted us. Then she and her husband John and their seven-year-old daughter, Catie, met us. Their dogs were a huge Weim, named Hershel, the puppy's father, a Rottweiler named Babe, and a twelve-week-old Weim puppy named Buster, which the family intended to keep. Catie went to get the puppy we were there to look at. Duane and our kids waited with bated breath to see the intended puppy. As Catie walked out with the small Weim puppy, we all instantly fell in love. "Runtski," as Catie called her, was adorable, small, and dark gray, very different from her massive brother, Buster, who was silver in color. Margaret said she was concerned about Runtski because she was sick. She had mucus coming out of her nose and around her huge golden eyes. Each of the kids held the puppy in turn and so did Duane and I, barely listening to Margaret's words of warning. Catie told us that she loved Runtski and wanted to keep her, but her mom said they couldn't keep two puppies. We heard another dog barking in the distance, and Margaret walked us over to a kennel with another Weim in it.

"This is Mackenzie, Runtski's mother. She is an alpha female and is aggressive with Babe. We are going to sell her." Everything was a blur because we only had eyes for Runtski. Duane and I walked away from the kids to make our decision about whether we should get this puppy. She was sick, but I thought, No big deal, she'll get better and she is cheap, only $100, a clearance dog. I told Margaret I'd take Runtski and promised Catie that I would take very good care of her. I also promised that I would send her pictures on the computer and got their email address. We said goodbye and thank you, watching Catie with tears in her eyes as we drove away.

We were heading back to our cabin and we were thinking up names. Sam wanted to name her Sparkle because, when the sun shined on her coat, she glistened. Colton thought we should name her Sapphire because she was a blue Weim. Duane thought she should be named Half Dome because she had a pointy-head. Amando and Alana thought of the name Sophie, and we all agreed that we liked it. She looked like a Sophie with her big golden eyes and soulful face. I thought that we should find out the Miwok name for Half Dome from a park ranger in Yosemite which I did. It is Tissiack. So, Sparkling Sapphire Sophia Tissiack is her formal name.

We brought her back to the cabin and all held her in turn. I noticed that I had to keep cleaning the mucus from around her eyes. The next morning her eyes were crusted together with mucus, and I had to gently wash it away. Then every hour I had to do the same thing.

We drove home to Livermore that day. I made a vet appointment for the next day. I brought Sophie to see Dr. Bloomfield, and she said she had no idea what was wrong with

Sophie and that I should make an appointment with a veterinary ophthalmologist in Fremont. The first vet appointment cost $95. Several days later, I took Sophie to see Dr. Smith, and she said Sophie had a rare condition called, puppy strangles. It is an allergic reaction to the strep bacteria in our environment. She would have to treat Sophie on a bi-weekly basis until Sophie was four months old, after all her shots, then she would be given a steroid called, Prednisone. After about $1,000 worth of vet bills, the vet finally cured our clearance dog.

Although we spent a small fortune on Sophie, we do not regret getting her. She has given us an immeasurable amount of love and affection, and that is priceless.

"Mommy, Where is Blue Jay?"

"Mommy, where's Blue Jay?" Sam asked.
"I don't know, Sam. Where's the last
place you had him?" I said.
"In my bed, in the loft."
"Okay, let's go find him, Sam."

Sophie and Sam at six

B lue Jay became part of our family two years
earlier. Sam and Blue Jay met one day
while we were buying snacks at a market in
Arnold. Duane, Sam, and I were on a day road
trip, looking for a cabin to purchase. Our goal
was to find the right area in the Sierra foothills
that met our needs. Duane loved the spicy scent
of pine trees, and I, on the other hand, was fond
of gnarled oaks.

We headed up Highway 4 to check out towns in Calaveras County: West Point, Andreas, Murphys, Arnold, and Dorrington. As we drove along the country roads, we discovered at 3,500 feet in elevation, both pine and oak trees shared the land in harmony. It was fall and the golden oak leaves shone like patches of sunlight amongst a sea of green sentinels.

The area around West Point was gorgeous, and the prices of properties were right, but as we drove around the little town, we noticed dilapidated homes with old rusty cars strewn about, and discarded household appliances littered the yards. Duane and I looked at each other, and I said, "I don't think this is the place for us. I want to have neighbors who take pride in keeping their yards clean."

We drove down to Murphys. It was a cute little town with nice shops. But it wasn't high enough in elevation and only had oak trees. We continued driving and found ourselves in Arnold. Sam was a real trooper. He was four years old and we had done a lot of driving that day. We were getting hungry and decided to stop and buy some snacks at the Big Trees Market. We were standing in line to buy chips, ice cream sandwiches, and soda when I saw a metal basket full of Beanie Babies. I said, "Sam, you have been such a good boy during our drive, why don't you pick out one of those Beanie Babies for yourself."

The display basket was full of the little plush stuffed animals. Different kinds of birds and mammals were mixed in a potpourri of color.

I walked over with Sam as he reached into the menagerie of animals, wading his little hand through the soft toys, not sure of what he wanted. Then he pulled out a bird with a snowy breast, sky blue wings, and crested head. "Mommy, I want this one. What kind of bird is this?" he asked, handing me the toy.

"It's a blue jay, Sam," I replied.

I looked at the label on the Beanie Baby and said to Sam, "His name is Rocket the Blue Jay. Are you sure you want this one? Why did you choose him?"

"Yes, Mommy, I'm sure. I like the thing on his head. What's that called?"

"Oh, that is called a crest," I replied.

We purchased blue jay and our snacks and drove up Highway 4, enjoying the beautiful scenery. We loved touring through Arnold and Dorrington, but when we saw the prices of the properties, we knew we couldn't afford them. Also, there were only pine trees. We drove back home feeling defeated as the sun set in the West.

Sam and Blue Jay became inseparable. The name Rocket never stuck. Sam had always been more of a literal child and referred to his Beanie Baby as Blue Jay. Sam took it everywhere. He slept, played, and ate with Blue Jay.

Now and then Sam would misplace Blue

Jay, and I got very good at finding the beloved toy. It got to the point that if I couldn't find Blue Jay before bedtime, Sam couldn't go to sleep. This scenario went on for two years.

We eventually found a listing of a cabin online in a little town called Greeley Hill in Mariposa County. The price was right, so we had made an appointment with a realtor the day after Thanksgiving of 2002. We had looked up the elevation of the town and it was listed at 3500 feet. *Perfect.* There should be oak and pine trees together, I thought happily to myself.

We met the realtor, Kathleen Love, at Coldwell Bankers in Greeley Hill, and we followed her to the cabin. It was on five acres of land covered with Live Oak, White, Cedar, Sugar Pine, and Yellow Pine trees. When we went inside the house, it opened into a large great room with a stone fireplace, vaulted ceiling, and huge windows that looked out upon the lovely trees. Duane and I looked at one another and smiled. Without saying a word, we knew we had found our cabin.

For the next year, we went to our cabin every other weekend and every holiday. Sam happily brought Blue Jay with him to keep him company. They had many adventures together outside among the trees, oak leaves, pine needles, and snow.

In 2004 we went up for Thanksgiving to our cabin. Amando, Colton, Sam, Alana, and Sophie, our dog, were with Duane and me. Sam had been up in the loft playing with Legos. He came down the stairs and said, "Mommy, where's Blue Jay?"

We looked everywhere in the cabin, under couches, under beds, in boxes, and rooms. Then we looked outside around the cabin. No Blue Jay. We searched all day and into the evening. No Blue Jay. Finally, it was bedtime, and I knew that Sam was going to have a difficult time sleeping, and he did. I read him a long story and he eventually fell asleep. Sam's siblings looked for Blue Jay the next several days and could not find him. We had to leave on Sunday to go back home and Sam was so upset, but there was nothing we could do. He had to learn to cope without Blue Jay. Sam was such a sensitive child and I worried about him and how he was going to deal with the situation.

Sam grieved for a while but eventually got over his loss. Several months later, we went to the cabin. I was vacuuming the couch and had taken the cushions off to vacuum underneath, and I found little clear plastic pellets, the kind that is inside Beanie Babies. I concluded Sophie our dog had eaten Blue Jay. It wasn't the first time Sophie had eaten unusual items. Here is a list of things she had eaten previously: Sam's socks, earplugs, rocks, tissue, and even one of my knee-high stockings. One day I expect to be out raking leaves around the cabin and find a shredded piece of sky-blue fabric, remnants of a digested Blue Jay.

The Anatomy Lesson

In 2006 I was giving an anatomy lesson to my primary class at Valley Montessori School in Livermore. Our school had purchased an interactive plastic mannequin about thirty inches in length, with removable organs. It had a head and torso, but no arms or legs. Half of the head came off to reveal the brain and I could remove one of the hemispheres and hold it in my hands. The torso was open in the front so that I could remove the heart, lungs, kidneys, liver, stomach, and intestines. It was a very popular item in our classroom.

One of the units we were studying at that time was the human body. I had given a lesson the previous day about the internal organs. I had taken out each organ and explained in simple terms its function and placed it back into the mannequin, showing its correct location in the body.

The next day during our morning circle time, I reviewed the organs of the human body with my students. I started with the brain and worked my way down. I asked the children sitting in a group, "Who can tell me what part of the human body this is?"

Morgan raised her hand and said, "Miss Mary, that's the brain."

"You are correct, Morgan. Please come and place the brain where it belongs."

Morgan, aged four, came and placed the brain carefully in the head of the mannequin. I then raised each organ, and the child who named the organ proceeded to place it in its correct area of the plastic body.

I came to the last internal organ to be placed back into the mannequin, and I asked the children, "What is the name of this internal organ?" I had the intestines in my hand. The classroom became quiet, and the children looked at each other with questioning looks on their faces. Then I gave them a hint. "This is the part of the body the food goes through before you poop."

That seemed to do the trick because one of my five-year-old boys raised his hand eagerly, with a big smile on his face.

"Yes, Calvin. What is the name of this organ?"

"Miss Mary, those are the intesticles!" he shouted out proudly.

With that answer, my co-teacher ran out of the room trying to hold back her laughter. I, on the other hand, had to keep a straight face, and as calmly as I could, I said to him, "Calvin, you are so close. They are called the intestines. Can you please come and place them into the mannequin?" He came up to me and grabbed the plastic intestines and put them in the correct spot.

During outside playtime, I told my co-teacher how unfair it was that she got to release her laughter, while I had to keep a straight face.

She said to me, "Mary, I don't know how you were able to keep from laughing. I was amazed."

At noon, when Calvin's mother came to pick him up, I quietly told her the story before I called him to the door. We giggled together. I said to her, "I have heard some funny words from my students in the past, but intesticles takes the cake."

The Fountain

Gazing out my kitchen window, mindlessly
washing dishes,
Aware of the lovely fountain outside on my
lawn.
Then I remember, remember the losses,
Jagged tears in my heart. Deaths of my loved
ones.
Tears in my eyes, feeling pain like a dull ache.
Grief, it is present, coursing through my veins.
It sinks in. Is this morbid? I disagree.
We must experience the sorrow to feel vibrantly
alive.
Quickly as the pain rushes in, it dissipates. I
sense relief.
Then I remember, remember the good times.
Feeling grateful for memories shared, never to
be taken away.

Pure love washes over me, my face turns up to
heaven,
Thanking God for my husband, children,
friends, and home.
Thankful for the fountain of life.

Seventh Heaven

Our Seventh Street house in 1933

I first came into being in the minds of a young couple named Thomas and Isabelle Scott, who married in 1881. Thomas attended law school and became the first attorney in Livermore. Amazingly, Isabelle also became an attorney, working alongside her husband in their law office on the corner of K and First Streets. They wanted a nice home to live in, to raise a family, so I became their focus for the next several years.

Thomas and Isabelle wanted me to be a comfortable residence and began searching for a piece of land in town. A half-acre lot was available on the corner of Seventh and J Streets that they were quite fond of, so they purchased it. The couple consulted with a contractor who drew up plans for my creation.

Redwood lumber was ordered from a mill in Willits, and windows ordered and glazed in

Oakland. My doors, hinges, and doorknobs were shipped from San Francisco. And so began my construction in early 1894. Masons constructed a lovely fireplace mantle and chimney, and the finishing carpenters created a wooden built-in china cabinet with glass doors in the dining room. My ceilings were built ten feet high in the parlor and dining room. Honey-colored oak flooring was laid throughout my rooms. A root cellar was dug, its door and staircase placed near the kitchen for convenience.

My construction was completed in the spring, and I looked stunning with my planked redwood siding and gleaming white paint. Thomas and Isabelle were happy to finally have me as their home. My dining room and parlor were furnished with an oak table, Victorian sofa, upholstered chairs, and a beautifully carved mahogany headboard in the bedroom.

A few years passed and Thomas and Isabelle had a son and named him Tom. Isabelle quickly became pregnant with another child and named her Eunice. Both Thomas's and Isabelle's mothers came to live under my roof too. They realized I wasn't big enough for their family anymore. A builder was consulted again, changing my attic into three bedrooms, and adding another fireplace to keep my upstairs warm. They also built a glorious sunroom along my east side as a place for their children to play.

The family lived happily within my walls until Thomas received a job offer in Bakersfield that he could not refuse. He packed up his entire family and headed south in 1905.

Moses and Eleanor Cole bought me from the Scotts and moved in shortly thereafter. They lived inside me for thirty-eight years and had a passel of children. They filled my walls with laughter, tears, and activity.

In 1933 a baby girl named Stephanie was brought to live with the Cole family by her mother, Julia Newman, who worked as a nurse at the tuberculosis sanatorium on Arroyo Road. When Stephanie was four years old, Julia married a man named Joseph Avilla. He was a hay truck driver in town. They eventually bought me from the Coles in 1943 for $2,000. Julia was then working at St. Paul's Hospital as a nurse a block away, on the corner of J and Eighth Streets. Stephanie was happy she didn't have to move. She liked sneaking upstairs and climbing out my east window and playing on the roof of my sunroom with her friend, Carole, while her parents were at work.

Stephanie went away to college to attend Sonoma State University and then married. Her parents lived in me for many years. Julia enjoyed gardening and lovingly tended to the rose bushes that were planted on my mowing strip. She always looked forward to having her grandchildren come to visit.

Julia died in 1981 and Joseph in 1990. I was too big for Stephanie to live in alone, so she decided to sell me and build a house right next door to me so I wouldn't feel lonely.

A woman named Mary Heaton had walked

the alphabetical and numbered streets in Livermore as a child and had noticed my cute structure and large garden. Then in 1991 when I was up for sale, she came inside with two of her children and her sister, Peggy, during an open house. At that time, Mary couldn't afford me; I needed too many repairs. She continued to think and dream about my rooms for many years. Little did she know that we would meet again.

I was sold to Dan and Bernie Donovan. The last hundred years, I had gotten a bit run down. I needed a new foundation, electrical wiring, new pipes, and a heating and cooling system. The Donovan's lived in me for eight years, but they found out that I was too much to take care of. I was sold to Joe and Lauren Pennesi.

The Pennesi's put a great deal of work into remodeling my kitchen with new cabinets and granite countertops and updated my bathrooms. I looked spectacular. They also built a garage with a room in the back that was used as a den. They had two children, Matt and Chloe. They changed the landscaping and added many shrubs and trees to my garden. The Pennesi's decided to move to a bigger house in town.

The Stark family bought me in 2004 and stayed for three years. They had two little girls at the time. They ran Page Mill Winery in town. They added several finishing touches like painting me a silvery green outside, adding gingerbread trim, and hanging wallpaper inside a few rooms. They, too, wanted a larger house for their growing family and moved to another home in Livermore.

On July 8, 2007, Mary Heaton drove down my street on a whim. It was her forty-fifth birthday. As she approached my corner, she saw that I was for sale. She pulled over across the street with tears in her eyes and called her husband and said, "Duane, my dream house is for sale. We have got to try to buy it."

"Mary, we can't afford that house," Duane said.

Miraculously, forty-five days later, the Heaton's moved into me. There was another family who offered more money to buy me, but I chose Mary and her family because she truly loves me. I was glad to have her three sons living in my rooms upstairs. She takes wonderful care of my garden and cleans my rooms inside and out. She enjoyed sharing my history with other people and volunteered to have me be a part of the Heritage Home Tour. Over 700 people walked through my walls on May 18, 2008. I was in all my glory being admired by so many people.

The Heaton's have lived inside me for seven years, and I want them to stay for a long, long, time. Mary and I have a very special connection: I am her "Seventh Heaven" because I am one of her favorite places in the whole wide world. I am one hundred and twenty years old, and I have to say, I look wonderful for my age.

Seventh Street house in 2016

I Love the Cabin

Duane and Mary at their cabin near Yosemite in 2005

I love to go to the cabin. It is a place where I can truly relax and enjoy spending time with my family. It is one hundred and sixteen miles from my home in Livermore to the cabin in Greeley Hill, a two and a half hour drive.

In the spring, there are wildflowers everywhere. I love to walk down to the pond and look for the many different species of bright flowers. While my sons and husband fish, I sit on the shore and look at the beautiful trees surrounding the pond.

A great blue heron lives at the pond. He roosts in a tall, dead tree on the edge of the water. I sit with my sketchbook and draw. The dragonflies skim over the pond, darting this way and that. Frogs leap in the reeds searching for bugs. Occasionally, I see a fish jump out of the water to catch a fly. The sky is a brilliant blue and puffy, white clouds skate across the sky.

In the summer, the earth is dry as toast at our cabin.

We enjoy sitting on our deck where the surrounding trees give us shade. The dappled sunlight is a relief as the intense summer heat bears down on us. When it gets too hot, we head for the swimming hole, which is about a 15-minute drive. After we get to our destination, we walk a mile to get to the creek. When it is 100 degrees outside, we are quite ready to get in the 60-degree snowmelt that comes from the Sierra Nevada mountain range. The tributary is the North Fork of the Merced River. There is a little waterfall that feeds into the swimming hole that we affectionately call Heaton's Hole.

I watch my children climb up the falls and jump down off the rocks. We bring snacks and drinks and spend the afternoon swimming and relaxing. After the refreshing swim, it's time to hike back to our car. We are all hot and dusty and ready for a barbecue back at the cabin.

In autumn, the leaves fall from the oak trees, and the air has a comforting earthy smell. The rain falls, and we can hear it beat on the roof. As the storm worsens, we see the lightning brighten the sky, and we count as we wait for the thunder to rumble. A fire burns in the pellet stove, and we read books or play Scrabble. The next morning, we get up and take our dog, Sophie, for a walk. The sky is clear and the air smells so fresh and clean that I drink it in.

In the winter, there is a definite chill in the air. The sky is dark, and it snows. We watch as the snow blankets the deck outside the sliding glass door in the evening, and we can't wait to see how much snow will fall during the night. The pellet stove keeps our cabin toasty warm and the night is quiet.

We wake up to a beautiful white winter scene. Outside, the trees and deck are covered with a foot of fresh snow. The kids suit up in their winter clothes and head out the door. I hear the whooping of voices as my sons and husband throw snowballs at one another. Then the sledding begins, and the goal is to make the perfect run.

I love to go to my cabin all year round. It is my sanctuary where I detox from the busy life I lead. Thank goodness I have somewhere to truly relax.

Unexpected Gift

Mary in her mom's faux fur coat and Duane

I t was Christmas Eve, 2008. Duane and our three sons were getting ready to pick up my mother and take her to dinner at Colleen's home. My father had died eleven years before, so we were usually the ones to drive Mom to holiday festivities.

My mom was eighty-one at the time. She had become frail from osteoporosis and weighed 110 pounds. While I was in my teens to my thirties, Mom had been about thirty pounds overweight, so I wasn't used to her being stick thin. It was difficult to see her emaciated. Her spine had many stress fractures and was bent like a twig covered with new-fallen snow.

Mom couldn't drive to Colleen's house because she had become blind from macular degeneration over the last fifteen years. Colleen, Katy, and I had taken care of her after our dad died, cooking, cleaning, shopping, and taking her to doctor's appointments. Pat was in a board and care facility because he was in the end stages of Parkinson's disease. Chris lived in Florida, and Mark lived in Reno and ran a restaurant. I was very grateful that I had the help of my sisters. I couldn't imagine doing everything for Mom by myself. I felt sorry for only children burdened with the full care of their aging parents.

We had arrived at Mom's house and I had a key, so I unlocked the door and we entered. Mom was sitting in her usual spot on the plaid living room couch, smoking a cigarette.

"Hi, Mom. Merry Christmas. Are you ready to go to Coll's?"

"Oh, hi, Mimi. Yes, I'm ready. Can you go upstairs to my closet and get my fur coat? It's going to get pretty chilly outside tonight, and I want to keep warm."

"Sure, Mom."

I ran up the stairs and entered her bedroom. I could see the open bedcovers on my mom's side of the bed. I looked at my dad's side where the blankets were left untouched. My father's absence still left a dull ache in my heart. I rounded the corner to the closet and found my mom's faux silver fox coat. When I was a kid, I sneaked into her closet to touch the variegated shades of smooth gray fur. I took it carefully off the hanger and put it on. It was quite heavy because it was long and went down to my mother's shins. On me, a child, it dragged on the floor. The inside of the garment was lined with shimmering dove gray satin embossed with a flowery pattern. I pretended to be a princess in that coat. It made me feel so grown up and regal.

I snapped out of my daydream, grabbed the fur, remembering my mother was waiting for me and walked downstairs.

"Mom, I have your coat. Can you stand up, please? I'll help you put it on."

My mom slowly pushed herself up from the couch and held her arms out. The fur enveloped her small stooped frame. I couldn't help being aware of the role reversal between my mother and me. Now she was the child and I the mother.

Once my mom was ready, I looped my arm through hers and gently guided her out of the house and into my van. I put her into the front passenger seat because it was easier for her to get in and out. Colleen's house was a ten-minute drive. Duane parked on the driveway so my mom wouldn't have far to walk.

I helped my mom out of the car and up to the house. I knocked on the wooden door and then opened it. Colleen knew we were arriving at four o'clock. She and I were the punctual ones in the family. She greeted us with a big smile and a long hug. She walked Mom into the family room and got her settled on the couch.

Katy was picking up Pat from the board and care home in Tracy. She lived in Manteca, and it made more sense for her to do it. Katy had been Mom's and Pat's main caregiver for the last twelve years. She was the most selfless person I knew. Katy, Pat, and her family arrived a half hour after us.

Colleen's house was always decorated beautifully with a Christmas tree and a train with a little town beneath it. Colleen is a perfectionist, and it was quite apparent by her immaculate home, lovely furnishings, and her sense of decor.

The house was alive with talking and laughter. It was good to be together as a family. I thought of Dad and Peggy who had died. It would never be the same without them, but I was grateful that the rest of my family was there. Colleen was a great cook, and I enjoyed the wonderful bounty of food. Several years ago, we decided as a family not to exchange presents. There were too many of us, and it was too costly to buy gifts for everyone. My mom had six children, fifteen grandchildren, and two great-grandchildren at the time. After dinner, we sang Christmas carols instead of opening presents. Then we ate dessert. Colleen always had an assortment of delicious Christmas cookies to choose from.

Around eight o'clock, my mom told me she was ready to go home. I got her coat and helped her put it on and guided her to my van. I gathered up my husband and three boys, and we took my mom home. I walked her into the house, and as I was helping her take off her fur, she said to me, "Mimi I want you to have my coat."

"What? No, Mom. Not yet. You should keep it. You'll need it."

"I want you to have the coat, Mimi. I don't wear it much anymore. You're my only daughter who seemed to like it, so I want you to have it."

"Are you sure, Mom?" My voice cracked as tears rolled down my cheeks.

"Yes, I am. Goodnight, Mimi. I love you. Thank you so much for everything you've done for me. You have been a good daughter."

"You're welcome. Mom. I love you so much." I gave her a long hug.

I cradled my gift as I watched my mom walk carefully upstairs holding on to the iron railing. She entered her bedroom and quietly closed the door. I stood for a moment, frozen. I knew this was going to be our last Christmas together. She had given me her precious fur coat. My mom had said goodbye to me.

Pat at seventeen

P at was eight years older than I, and Mom told me he grew slowly and did not talk until three years of age. She was concerned about Pat, so she took him to the doctor and he ordered some tests and discovered Pat had a heart defect. The doctor said unless Pat had surgery to correct it, he would not live to adulthood. Open heart surgery was in its infancy in the early 60s, but my parents decided it was worth the risk. The surgery was performed at UCSF and was successful. Pat was in the hospital for a month and Mom and Dad visited him on the weekends. Pat told me how lonely he was during his convalescence.

My first memory of Pat was when we moved to Livermore because he got the entire basement to himself. Since he was the oldest son, he got his own room. I am pretty sure the rest of my siblings were envious too.

Pat loved to collect things: stamps, coins, rocks, record albums, CDs, music books, and model trains. He was a quiet person who liked to spend time by himself. The kids in our neighborhood described him as "different." He did not go outside and play with the rest of us. He preferred staying inside with his collections and building a model train town.

Pat was shy, but his behavior changed when he had to do his chores. He hated washing the dishes, so he banged and clanged the pots and pans and complained out loud. It used to scare me. The rest of us kids did not like doing chores, but we accepted our jobs and silently worked at our tasks.

We all had jobs to do around the house. When I was five, I used to set the table for dinner, Mark cleared the plates, Chris took out the garbage, and Katy, Pat, Peggy, and Colleen took turns doing the dishes. We had a huge family, and we all had to pull our weight.

A month before Pat's thirteenth birthday, he received an electric guitar for Christmas. I could not believe he got such an expensive gift. I guess he must have asked for a guitar, and I did not know it. Pat took lessons and eventually played well. He spent a lot of time in the basement practicing. It drove my mom and dad crazy when turned up the amplifier, so Dad yelled, "Patrick, turn that damn thing down."

Mom said to me, "I wish Pat would finish an entire song. He only plays parts of songs." I tended to agree with her. I wanted to hear a full song too.

After I had played the flute for several years, Pat and I played "Colour My World" by Chicago together, I on my flute and he on the guitar. I really enjoyed playing that song with Pat. It sounded beautiful.

As I got older, I noticed more differences between Pat and the rest of my siblings. He did not have many friends. He did not go to college, and he worked at jobs where he did not have to deal with the public, like being a dishwasher, cook, and printer. He never had a girlfriend, but I knew he liked girls because he had *Playboy* magazines in his room. I knew this because I discovered the magazines while looking for music books.

Pat moved out of our parents' home twice, but both experiences failed after a few years because his roommates got girlfriends and Pat ended up moving back home. I felt bad for him. He was in his thirties the last time moving out failed, and he just stayed with Mom and Dad.

Pat never married and did not have children, but he adored his nephews and nieces, all fifteen of them. He was the photographer in the family and took pictures at all the family gatherings. Pat was a generous person who bought thoughtful birthday gifts for each one of us. When I was single after my divorce, Pat came from Livermore to Fremont and babysat my three kids so I could get out of the house and have some fun. He helped me out and I was very grateful.

When I began teaching at Valley Montessori School, I had several students with social difficulties and delayed speech. To help those children, I read articles and books about the autistic spectrum. After years of noticing Pat was "different," I concluded he may have had Asperger's Syndrome, but had never been diagnosed. Pat was born in 1954 and there was not a lot of research or testing then. Pat was highly functioning and quite intelligent. It explained his lack of social interaction, temper tantrums, and connecting more with objects than people.

In his mid-thirties, Pat got a job in a warehouse loading freight onto railcars in Livermore. He seemed to like that job because he loved to be around trains. After a few years, he injured his shoulder and tore his rotator cuff. He had surgery, but it did not appear to be successful because he still had problems raising his left arm.

Pat began having tremors in his left hand and went to his doctor to get checked out. The doctor noticed Pat had other symptoms and diagnosed him with Parkinson's disease at the age of forty-one. We were all devastated to hear the news. Pat was young, and we thought Parkinson's was an old person's disease. Our

Uncle Elmer, our dad's brother, had it, but he was in his seventies.

Pat went on disability and spent time with his collections. He had two great friends, Mike Daly and Malcolm Bankhead. They picked him up once a month and took him to the movies or out to dinner. They were so kind to Pat.

After Dad died in 1997, Pat and Mom continued to live together. Mom was going blind, so Pat managed to heat food for them. They kept each other company. Mark lived with Mom and Pat for a few years and helped Pat if he fell. Then Mark moved to Reno, and Pat's symptoms got worse. Pat fell in the house, and Mom had to call Duane to come to pick him up. It was getting too dangerous for Pat to stay there.

The rest of us siblings got together and discussed the best options for Pat's care. We felt it was time for him to live in a board and care facility. Katy did the research and visited different homes. Colleen and I went to a few of them to help Katy decide which one was the best. She had found one in Tracy that was nice. It cost more than Pat's disability paid, so each of us chipped in money each month so Pat could live in a quality board and care home.

After two years, Pat began to lose the ability to swallow. He had to have a PEG put into his stomach so he could get nutrition through a feeding tube. Pat had to go into a convalescent hospital and he hated it. Within two months Pat had deteriorated to the point where hospice was needed.

Katy found a wonderful place called Hospice of San Joaquin located in Stockton. We all took turns being with Pat. The nurses there were angels on earth, so kind and caring. For some reason, I began to sing to Pat when I went to see him. I think it is because we always had a musical connection. I knew how much Pat loved music, and I wanted to do something to bring him comfort at the end of his life.

I had arrived home from the hospice on June 16, 2009, when I received a call from Katy telling me Pat had just died, and I wept. That night was my first writing class with Susan Wilson. I wasn't sure if I should go or not, but a voice told me I needed to attend the class. I think it was Pat urging me to write.

I came home later in the evening and shared my class experience with Duane. We were in our hot tub, and as we spoke of Pat's death, I heard an owl screech. We looked up to see an owl flying above us. The owl was illuminated by light, but I could not figure out the source. It was a peculiar sight because instead of the owl flying over us, it flew straight up into the heavens. I believe it was my brother's spirit saying goodbye, and it gave me a sense of peace. Pat had had a difficult life, and I am glad that he was finally at rest.

Mom and Dad dancing in 1960

"Hey Mom, it's me." I slowly opened the front door of my childhood home with a key.

"Hi, Mimi. How are you? Can you come to the living room and talk with me? I have something important to tell you."

"Ok, Mom. I'll put the groceries away later." I set the bags down on the oak table and walked into the living room where my mom sat on the plaid sofa. I sat across from her in my dad's old La-Z-Boy recliner.

241

"Mimi, last night your dad came to visit me."

"He did? Wow, that's wonderful, Mom."

"He walked into my room and stood at the end of the bed for a bit. The light of the full moon was streaming in from the window, and I could see he was wearing his Naval officer's uniform. Gosh, he looked so handsome, it took my breath away."

"Oh, Mom, that's amazing. I am so happy he came to visit. You haven't seen him in twelve years. I know how much you've missed him. Did he say anything to you?"

"No, he came over and sat on the edge of the bed. He took my left hand in his and smiled at me. I could feel the warmth of his skin on mine. He touched my gold wedding band and twirled it around my ring finger."

My mother's face beamed while she spoke to me. Tears began to collect in my eyes, and I smiled.

"Mom, I am so glad Dad came to visit. It won't be long now before you can be with him all the time. Are you ready, Mom, to be with Dad?"

"Yes, I'm ready Mimi. It won't be long now. I've missed him terribly."

"I know you have. It will be a blessing for you to be together again."

"Did you say anything to Dad?"

"Yes, I told him I love him, and I will be joining him soon, and he squeezed my hand. Then he bent down to kiss me, and his form cast a moon shadow across my face. I felt his soft lips touch mine. I feel so giddy, like a schoolgirl who just got her first kiss."

I laughed and walked over to the couch to give my mom a long hug.

"I love you so much, Mom. I'm going to miss you, but I know why you want to leave."

"I'm glad you understand. I don't think your sisters and brothers do. That's why I am only telling you about Dad's visit. Can you keep it to yourself?"

"Sure, Mom, I will. Now, can I get you something to eat?"

"Yes. Did you buy me a Boston Cream Pie like I asked? That's all I want. A huge piece of it."

"Yes, Mom, I got you a Boston Cream Pie. It was the last one at Safeway. I'll go cut you a piece and bring you a big cup of milk to go with it."

I went into the kitchen and cut a piece of pie for my mom and poured her some milk. I grinned, but tears ran down my cheeks. It's such a strange feeling to be extremely happy and profoundly sad at the same time. *I'm forty-seven years old. I can deal with Mom leaving to be with Dad. They should be together. I can't be selfish. I want Mom and Dad to be happy.* I walked back to the living room with her snack. I placed the food on a wooden TV tray in front of the couch next to my mom.

"Here you go, Mom. Your pie is right in front of you on the TV tray. Your spoon is to the right of your bowl, and your cup of milk is at eleven o'clock. Enjoy."

She slowly reached out and touched the wooden stand. She felt for the china bowl with her left hand. She reached her right hand and felt for the metal spoon. She used the fingers of her left hand to gently touch the pie, scooped some of it up with her spoon, put it in her mouth, and chewed.

"Oh, Mimi, thank you for getting me Boston Cream Pie. It's my favorite. So yummy."

"Sure, Mom. Anything to make you happy."

I watched her while she ate. I was amazed at how well she could eat without help. She polished off her chocolatey, creamy treat quickly.

"That was delicious. I wonder if they have Boston Cream Pie in heaven?"

"Well, I don't think you're going to need food in heaven, Mom."

"I wonder if I will be able to see there. What do you think, Mimi?"

"I think you will. You saw Dad last night, didn't you?"

"That I did, that I did." She lay back on the couch and sighed contentedly.

Three months later, on Labor Day weekend, I received a call at the cabin. It was Colleen. She said, "Mary, I went to check on Mom at her house because when I called her yesterday morning, she did not answer. I went to the house right away and when I arrived, I called her name and I could hear her voice from up in her bedroom. I went into the room and she had fallen. I need you to come home and help me take care of her. I called Aunt Jane and she will be here in a few days."

My mother had a series of small strokes. Three weeks later, she passed away on September 20th. I was happy she was reunited with my father.

Marky

Marky at seventeen

D earest Marky,

I have been thinking a lot about you and how difficult life has been. As we both know, life is very transient. I wanted to let you know how much I care for you because you never know what will happen. I want to share some of my memories with you, and you will probably remember some of them too.

All my earliest memories have you in them. You were my first best friend and protector. You were the buffer between Mom and me and Chris and me. You were the quiet, easy-going, child, and I, the emotional and extremely sensitive child. A sister who was highly sensitive to sound, light, and emotion.

I remember being a three-year-old in the

backyard when a plane flew over and I cried and you told me it would be gone soon. Do you remember getting a chair from the house so we could pick the cherries off the tree? I remember many of them were unripe. Remember when I fell off the teeter-totter at the house and got a black eye? Those are the memories I have of San Lorenzo.

Remember when we went to New York with Mom? It was a big deal. I remember getting on the plane and crying so hard because I was scared and didn't want to leave Dad, but having you there made me feel better. I remember being on the Staten Island ferry and eating Cracker Jacks with you and hearing the tugboats and watching them push the big ships. I remember seeing Nana Claffy at the hospital and feeling scared. I remember leaving Nana's house, and you had something in your pocket. I asked what you had, and Mom asked you to take it out, and we saw you had taken Papa's match boot. It was a small bronze boot that held matches. I remember being at Cousin Kathleen's house and going into her attic and her giving me a little stuffed horse, white with blue flowers and a yellow mane and tail. At the dinner table, I forgot to say please and Aunt Jane scolded me and I was afraid of her in her nun's habit.

When we moved to Livermore, it was so different. I remember all the fun we had exploring in the fields. I was so sad when you went to school. I couldn't wait until you got home. I was so lonely when you were gone because Mom was depressed and didn't talk much.

I was ecstatic when I got to go to school. We made other friends and our lives changed. We were still friends, but you were a boy and I was a girl, so it was inevitable. I still preferred to hang out with you guys, playing sports. You were always good about letting me play. I really appreciated that.

I always remember feeling connected to you. When you fell off your bike that time and bumped your head, I was so worried. The time you broke your arm on the monkey bars. I liked that we were only one year apart, "Irish twins." I felt so safe at school knowing you were there to help me if I needed it. No one bothered me at school because they knew you were my brother. I especially liked that we were at Junction together; it was kind of scary going to middle school. I remember at the dances, dancing with you when no one else asked me. There was a picture taken of us before a dance. I was in seventh grade and you in eighth and we were the same height. I wonder where that picture is. And then, of course, you shot up in height. You went from a skinny kid to a good-looking guy and by 16, all the girls liked you. I was always (and still am), critical of the girls you date. And I never got asked out in high school because of you. In hindsight, it was for the best.

It was also great working at the Livermore Railway together and hanging out as a group. It cracked me up that Mom felt I was safe because you were with me, but it should have been the other way around. Do you remember when we wanted to go to the movies one night and Mom was in one of her dark moods? She told us we couldn't go and you walked out the door, defying her! I couldn't believe you did that. And that was the end of the control she had over you. From that point on, you did what you wanted to do. Then you graduated from high school and went off to Reno to work. And since then, we haven't seen a whole lot of each other, living our own lives. In 1983 you came to visit. I had a party at my house in Sunol, and you told me your girlfriend was pregnant. You asked my advice on when to tell the family, and I said the sooner the better. That was difficult for you, but it was better to tell everyone at the same time. Then you got married and then I got married. We were busy with our families which both ended in heartache for different reasons.

I have always felt your pain in those difficult times. Is it because we came from the same womb? I don't think so, because I don't feel the same way with any of our other siblings. We have a special bond; we are each other's barometers. In the last thirteen years, we have lost so much. First, Mike taking his own life. There was nothing you could do. You were his friend, and he loved you so much. He had his own demons, and you couldn't stop them. Then we lost Dad. I am so thankful that you were there when he passed. Then we lost Peggy. My heart still aches for her presence. I miss her so much. Then our dear friend Ray, your best friend, died. What a shock. I will never forget when you called and told me. I remember the raw, aching wound it left in you. Then our poor, generous brother Pat, who never had a good break in his life. Then Mom, her frail little body, so ready to be with Dad. Then your dog Jack, a wonderful companion. I have felt all your pain and feel it still.

You are so great at being a restaurateur and chef. You have a charisma that people are drawn to and want to be around. You are a wonderful songwriter and musician. The greatest gift you have is that you make people laugh. That's what Mom so loved about you; you always made her laugh.

Marky, I don't know which one of us will go first, but I do know that if you do, the loss I will feel will be immeasurable. And the grief will be deep and long. And the sun's light will not be as bright. If I go first, I will be waiting very impatiently in heaven with Mom, Dad, Peg, Pat, Ray, and Mike, for you to join us so we can celebrate your arrival.

I love you more than words can say,
Happy Birthday, Marky!
Love your little sister, Mary 5/2/2010

The Toast

Mary, Aunt Jane, Colleen, and Katy

I was in a perky mood on the morning of April 29, 2011. Duane and I were driving from Livermore to North Lake Tahoe to celebrate my brother, Mark's fiftieth birthday. I was afraid it might snow, which is always a possibility during late spring in the Sierras, but we lucked out and the day was gorgeous a crystal-clear cerulean sky.

All my siblings were meeting at the Rustic Cottages in Tahoe where the event was being held. Chris flew from Florida, and Aunt Jane flew from New York to attend the celebration. Katy and Colleen drove up with their husbands from the Bay Area. Each of us couples and aunt had booked a cottage months before. Chris was going to stay in the main house with Mark. And I am sure my Mom, Dad, Peggy, and Pat were there in spirit.

Duane and I arrived around 3:00 p.m. and asked the innkeeper where the main house was located on the property. As we walked there, my sisters and aunt arrived. After we greeted each other warmly, we went in search of Mark. We found my brother in the rental house, noticing quickly that he was already feeling merry, a vodka-grapefruit grasped in his hand.

Our group left Mark and his friends and went for a walk in the neighborhood to catch up with one another before we started to party. Since it was such a lovely day, we strolled down to the lake, admiring its beauty, and stood letting the warmth of the sun soak into our bodies as we watched sailboats drift across the sparkling water. We trudged back to the cottages, our breaths labored from the effects of the high altitude.

It was close to 5:00 p.m. and we rejoined Mark to celebrate. I made Tanqueray martinis for my sisters, our husbands, and myself. Mark's daughter, Megan, made a Cosmopolitan for Aunt Jane. We happily chatted with each other as we watched Mark open his birthday gifts.

A few months before, I sent emails to my siblings asking if they would chip in money for a gift for Mark, a DNA test, and membership to 23andme. At first, my sisters resisted. They thought it wasn't personal enough, but their husbands thought it was a great idea and changed their wives' minds, so I sent for the kit. I had my DNA tested a few years before, and because I am a woman, I couldn't find out information about my paternal DNA unless Mark got his DNA tested too. It was a win-win deal. All the siblings would benefit from the gift.

I handed the present to Mark at his party and when he opened it, I said, "Mark, it's a DNA test for you. Now, we can get all the DNA results to find our ancestry."

"Wow, that's great, Mare. But I don't think this is the time or place to give a sample of my DNA" he said with a smirk.

"Marky, you don't give that kind of sample," I replied, laughing. "Here is the tube you just spit in it, and I will send it in. Four weeks from now, your DNA report will be sent to your computer."

"Gimme that thing," Mark said, grabbing the plastic vial from me. He proceeded to slowly spit into the tube, the rest of us giggling. "Well, I don't know how accurate it's gonna be because it's got to be mostly alcohol goin' into this thing," he said, handing it back to me.

"We'll find out in about a month, and the company said if they can't get a good reading of the DNA, they will send another kit," I said reassuringly.

Mark opened the rest of his presents, modeling the hats and clothes he received, making us all laugh. Each of us siblings played individual roles in our family: Mark, the comedian, Colleen, the businesswoman, Peggy, the hippy, Pat, the hobbyist, Katy, the caregiver, Chris, the imp turned born-again Christian, and me, the baby, the sentimental storyteller. I had also taken on the role of the toast giver at celebrations since our mom died. I have been told by my family that I remind them a lot of my mother in this regard.

We were all having a grand time, helping set the table outside, and putting the food out. There were about thirty guests. Since Mark ran a restaurant, he and his employees had prepared a feast fit for a king holding court: baby back ribs, Caesar salad, grilled veggies, baked potatoes, warm sourdough bread, and lots of Pinot Noir, my brother's favorite wine.

The sun was setting behind the majestic mountains as we gathered outside on the deck to be seated. Once we all had food and drink, I stood up and proposed a toast to Mark. I raised my wine glass but noticed it was empty. Instead of refilling it, I used it as a makeshift microphone, speaking into it while I gave my speech.

"Tonight, we are all here to celebrate Marky's fiftieth birthday."

Everyone cheered and applauded.

"I just want to say that I love my brother so much. He was my first best friend and protector. We are only fourteen months apart, almost Irish twins, but thank God, not really, for my mother's sake. I propose a toast to honor my brother. May he have many more years to come."

With the last word, I raised my wine glass cheering to all. I set my glass down on the table, maybe a tad harder than normal, and it shattered to pieces.

Pandemonium broke loose and the thirty guests including me laughed hysterically. My sisters, aunt, and I couldn't even breathe, tears running down our cheeks. It took several minutes before everyone calmed down. I realized at that moment I had finally upstaged Mark for the first time in my life. It felt great.

The next morning, I woke up in our little cottage, laughing all over again about the night before. Duane looked at me and said, "Mary what the heck is so funny?"

"Last night, when I broke my wine glass, of course."

"Yeah, that was hilarious." He chuckled.

We dressed and walked up to the lodge to have breakfast with my family. Duane and I arrived first, pouring us a cup of coffee. Katy came in. "Mary, I woke up laughing. That was the best night ever," she said, smiling.

And that is the fondest memory I have of Katy that I will keep tucked in my heart forever.

Katy at twenty-one

Katy was the fourth child born to Kate and Dick Hansen. She was six years older than I. Katy had a blonde bob and a beautiful smile that lit up her face. She had clear blue eyes, and when I looked into them, I knew she was a truly good person. Katy was an angel that lived on this earth and took care of others selflessly every day. She was my sister and my best friend.

When my family moved to Livermore in 1966, Katy and I shared a room in the new house. I remember lying there on our beds. We were so excited to be in a new house, and it smelled like wood and new paint. We could hear the cars in the distance from the Lincoln Highway.

I was her pesky little sister, and I tried to hang around her when she was home, but she wasn't home much. She was always busy doing something at school. She was in the student government and an excellent student. Katy was very outgoing and popular with her classmates. At seventeen, Katy had long, blond hair and a great figure. She had several boyfriends in high school and many more guys who wished they were.

When Katy was eighteen, she went away to college at Humboldt State University. Katy was very excited about going to college, but it was very difficult for me. I was twelve years old, and Colleen and Peggy had already left. I was the only girl at the house with three brothers. My only consolation was that I got my own room.

Katy was at Humboldt State College for two years and then came home. She was quite homesick, which surprised me. She always seemed so confident, but she was a very sensitive young woman. During her time at college, she became a born-again Christian. This completely changed her life. From that point on, she lived a purely Christ-like life.

Katy began taking classes at Cal State Hayward and met a young man named Tim. My sister fell head over heels in love with him and was married within seven months. She was twenty-one years old when she married. She asked me to be her maid of honor, and I was thrilled. I was fifteen years old at the time. Katy and Tim moved to an apartment in San Leandro for about a year, and then they moved to Chicago because Tim decided to go a Bible College to study theology. They were gone for four years. I really missed Katy during that time.

Katy gave birth to two children in Chicago, Joshua and Caleb. They were less than two years apart, and she had her hands full. I wished she had lived closer so I could have helped her. Mom never did go to visit her, and that made Katy sad.

Katy came back to California in 1983, and I was so happy. Katy gave birth to another boy in 1985 and named him Dawson. He was a very cute boy with thick, strawberry blonde hair and big blue eyes. He was an extremely active child, and Katy had her hands full with three sons.

In 1986 Katy became pregnant with her fourth child, and I became pregnant with my first. It was so much fun being pregnant at the same time. I called Katy often to ask her for advice. She and I became close at that time.

On January 23, 1987, Katy gave birth to Katelyn Ann. Five days later at the same hospital, I gave birth to Alana Maria. Katy was being discharged the day I went into the hospital. She came into my labor room and stayed with me for a couple of hours to give my husband a break. She was so sweet and loving to me while I was having labor pains.

Our daughters grew up together. I lived in Fremont and Katy lived in San Leandro. We tried to get together often. I went over there because it was easier for her. Then, I had two boys, and it was much more difficult to see her. We saw each other on all the special occasions. We always spoke on the phone to keep in touch.

In 1996 Katy and her family moved to Manteca. Katy homeschooled all her children. She was a very devoted mother. Joshua and Dawson had ADHD and she felt they would not do well at school and it would become a behavioral problem. I was amazed by her patience with her children and her dedication.

She seemed indefatigable.

Her children went to public high school, and they all were excellent students. They all attended the University of Pacific and graduated with honors. Katy was proud of all her children's accomplishments.

Dawson was a consummate musician and played the guitar beautifully. After college, he became a music teacher and gave guitar lessons. When he was twenty years old, there was a change in his personality. But he seemed to bounce back, and he finished college.

Katy had been taking care of Pat and Mom. She cleaned their house and cooked meals. Katy took them to doctors' appointments and helped them with their medication. She was a loving and giving sister and daughter. Pat died in June of 2009 and Mom in September the same year. Katy was devastated.

Meanwhile, Dawson's problems got worse and Katy tried to help him. She took him to several doctors because he had mental problems. He began feeling intense pain, and

Katy took him to Stanford in September 2011 to get him help. She was disappointed because she didn't feel they helped Dawson at all.

Katy was very worried about her son. She brought him to a psychiatrist and got him medication. His behavior had changed drastically, but Katy kept Dawson's behavior from us. She knew it would upset us. Tim traveled away from home many weeks that year. She dealt with Dawson's issues alone. Tim and Dawson did not get along.

I saw Katy that September, and we had lunch with Colleen. We had the best time laughing and going to find a dress for Katy for Katelyn's wedding, on December 17, 2011. Katy was beaming and couldn't wait to see her daughter get married. We were so happy for her.

The Unspeakable

On Halloween night 2011, Colleen called me at 6:35 p.m. I had just handed out candy to the first trick or treaters, Minnie Mouse and Captain Hook.

"Mare, it's Coll. Joshua just called me. Katy is dead."

"What? How can Katy be dead? I don't understand. How did she die?"

"Joshua doesn't know. Please come over." She hung up the phone.

Duane was sitting on the loveseat in our living room and had heard what I said. He jumped up and ran over to me and held me tightly as I sobbed. My body went into spasms. I could barely move. Katy was my beloved sister and now she was dead.

"Duane, we need to go to Colleen's. I have to be with her right now."

Duane drove me to Colleen's house a mile away, and we speculated over Katy's cause of death. Did she have a heart attack, stroke, or an aneurysm? We talked for a few hours and comforted one another. We had to wait for the autopsy.

Two days later, Joshua called Colleen and told her that Dawson had murdered Katy, their mother. The police then searched for Dawson and found him in his car in a parking lot a mile from his house. They had taken him to jail.

I was devastated again.

During the last year when I had seen Katy, she described Dawson's disturbing behavior. He had become antisocial and lost his job. He was an amazing guitar player but had stopped playing. He began wearing masks. I was very concerned about him. I was extremely worried about Katy. It was causing her a great deal of stress. She was trying to get Dawson help by taking him to various doctors. Tim stayed away from home as much as possible. He was a computer parts salesman and traveled to China for weeks at a time and left Katy to deal with their son.

Dawson was in jail for a year. No one in his immediate family ever went to visit him. Duane and I went to the San Joaquin County Jail in Angels Camp twice to see Dawson, but he refused to see us.

From My Heart

Mary at her college graduation from
Cal State Hayward in 1990

I have read that public speaking is the greatest fear people have. They fear it more than death. I used to be one of those people, but I am not anymore.

My first memory of speaking in public occurred in seventh grade while I was giving an oral report on the history of the American flag. I remember standing in front of my social studies class terrified, my pulse racing, and my face the color of a ripe tomato. I tried to talk, but my voice kept cracking. I was finally able to get through my report, but it was a very traumatic experience for me.

When I was fourteen years old, I got a job at the Old Livermore Railway, a restaurant where Pat, Katy, Chris, and Mark, four of my siblings, worked. I was first hired as a cornbread girl, a job where I had to walk around the dining room asking the patrons if they would like some cornbread and honey butter. This was difficult at first, but then, with practice, it was a piece of cake, or I should say, a piece of cornbread.

After about a year at that job, I was ready to move up in the ranks. I asked my manager if I could become a hostess, and before I knew it, I got my wish. That job was much more difficult. It required strategic planning of where to seat guests. It was a family-style restaurant, and the menu changed nightly, so to save on paper, the owners required the hostess to recite the menu at each table as she seated the customers. That was so much harder than I imagined. But again, after much practice, it became easier.

As I entered college, I needed more money and again, I needed to move up the ranks of the restaurant. I became a server. Talk about a difficult job. I still have nightmares from that experience. I had to remember drink orders, dinner orders, and multitask. It was a two-story restaurant, and I had to carry heavy trays of food up and down a back staircase. I had never worked so hard, or so I thought then. That is how I put myself through college.

NEVER A DULL MOMENT

In my senior year of college, I set a goal. I was determined to speak at my graduation. It was a personal achievement that I wanted to attain to prove how far I had come from my fear of public speaking. I wasn't sure how I was going to finagle it, but I was going to try.

The last semester of college was very busy, and I was caring for a baby and a toddler to boot. Connie, a fellow student asked me if I could arrange for someone to speak at graduation. I couldn't believe my luck. I said, "Can I speak at the graduation?" And she said, "Yes, Mary, that would be great."

So with commencement quickly approaching, I asked myself, what have I gotten myself into? I never used a paper at work to read from, so why use one now? I gave it a lot of thought and decided that if I speak from my heart, I could not fail. So, I imagined the chapters of my life and my experiences in college that meant so much to me and memorized them. I felt that if I could look at the audience and connect with them and speak from my heart, then the message I wanted to convey would be more powerful.

I was excited on the night of my graduation. I made sure my parents and all six of my brothers and sisters were there. What an act of God that was. My parents never went anywhere, and I had to get Mark to drive them from Livermore to Hayward and back home. I was the first of seven children to graduate from college, and I was the baby. I was proud to have my entire family there to hear me speak.

When Ann Meyer, the head professor of the Department of Human Development, called my name, my heart beat faster. I walked up to the podium and looked out over the thousand-plus people. I spoke calmly and with grace about my journey up to that time, and it came out perfectly. No cracking of my voice, no stammering. I felt elated when I was done. The last line of my speech was, "There is one person here tonight that is extremely proud of me and that person is . . . me." I was the one who did all the college work, waitressed in a restaurant, and took care of my children.

When I think back to that evening long ago, I am still amazed that I was able to accomplish my goal. Since then, I have spoken at many school events and memorial services including Katy's service.

Katy's spirit came to me after she died and told me that I needed to stand up for her son. She said, "Mary, no one else will speak for Dawson. You must have the courage to stand up for him." I knew that I needed to do what she asked. I stood in church and spoke the truth, and it was from my heart. I spoke about my relationship with my sister, and then I said, "There are two things I know with certainty, that Katy is in heaven, and she has forgiven her son. And to heal our hearts, we must forgive him. It is what Katy wants, and it is what God wants."

It took a lot of courage for me to say those words to all those people, and I know I touched many hearts that day. After the memorial, people who knew Katy came up to me and told me she would be so proud of me. My heart swelled with love for my sister and her son. And I felt certain that I had done right by them.

Stand Up

D awson's trial began on November 2, 2012, and lasted two months. January 28, 2013, was the day of his sentencing. I paced up and down the dingy hallway of the Stockton Courthouse, waiting to speak in front of the judge to tell him my observations that led up to Katy's murder. Duane stood ten feet down from the courtroom door watching me with a concerned look. He had been my steadfast supporter these two months of hell. I walked over to him and held his hand. My palm was sweaty and my hand was shaking. I gazed down the hallway noticing my nephew, Joshua, walking toward us.

"Hi, Aunt Mary and Uncle Duane."

"Hi, Joshua," I said.

"Well, I have been waiting for this day for over a year. I am going to read the lyrics to the songs I wrote about the defendant."

I winced when I heard Joshua call his brother, Dawson, the defendant. It unnerved me to witness the lack of compassion that Joshua had for his mentally ill brother.

"Aunt Mary, are you going to say anything to the judge today?"

"Yes, Joshua I am. I would like to go last if that's okay with you."

"Are you sure? I wanted to go last. My songs are brilliant. They should be the encore. Aunt

Mary, do you know what an encore is? I don't think you should follow me because I am going to blow away everyone in the courtroom with what I read."

"Yes, Joshua, I know what encore means. Don't worry about me. I have confidence in myself. Whatever you say will not take that away. I would still like to speak last."

I knew that Tim, Joshua, and Rebecca, Joshua's wife, were all going to speak with condemnation towards Dawson, while I was going to speak of forgiveness. That's what Katy would want from me.

Tim walked toward me with a blonde woman in tow. I asked Joshua, "Who is that person with your dad?"

He smirked. "Oh, that's my dad's new friend. I will let him introduce her."

Tim walked up to us and said, "Mary and Duane, I would like to introduce you to my fiancée Penny. We are getting married in two weeks on Valentine's Day."

I stood stock-still. My heart pounded like a sledgehammer in my chest. I was appalled at Tim's words. He claimed to be a devout Christian, but his actions proved otherwise. *How dare he bring a woman to his son's sentencing? What kind of person does that?*

Blood steamed in my veins as I reluctantly shook the woman's hand. Tim's latest atrocity gave me even more courage to stand in front of Judge Johnston and speak the truth about events that led up to Katy's death.

It was 10:30 a.m. when the bailiff opened the courtroom doors. We filed into the room and took our places. Duane and I sat on the right side of the gallery behind Dawson and his defense attorney, while Tim, Penny, Joshua, Rebecca, her father, and a few of their friends sat behind the prosecutor. It was similar to the seating arrangements at a wedding.

Tim spoke to the court first. His words did not affect me negatively because I knew he was going to blame his son and not address his negligence in this tragedy.

Rebecca was the next person to speak. She took the book, *The Giving Tree,* and made a parody of the story, changing it to The Taking Tree. She depicted how Dawson manipulated Katy to do his bidding.

Then Joshua got up to read the lyrics to three songs he wrote about his brother. It was more of a theatrical performance than a heartfelt cathartic speech. They all read from scripts.

Then the judge called my name. I walked up to the podium. I felt jittery, but then a wave of calm washed over me, and I spoke in a loud, clear voice, so everyone in the courtroom could hear me. I could see Dawson in my peripheral vision wearing a blue shirt and gray slacks. I was not allowed to face him directly.

"Your Honor, I felt compelled to speak today on my sister, Katy's, behalf. You see, she and I were very close. She was six years older, and we shared a room for twelve years while we were growing up. We were even at the hospital at the same time when she gave birth to her last child and me to my first. We called each other often and shared holidays. She was a devoted mother to all of her children. She took her job seriously. She was a compassionate woman.

"Your Honor, I also need to clarify a few events to the court. I believe that we would not be present today if Tim had done his job as a husband and father. You heard testimony that Tim went on business trips to China. What you didn't hear was that Tim was in China 180 days the last year of Katy's life. While she was trying to seek help for their mentally ill son, Tim was absent. She was virtually a single parent."

"Back in February of 2011, I went out to dinner with Katy and Tim. He told me he had been sleeping with one eye open because he was afraid of his son. Your Honor, if Tim was afraid for his own life, why did he leave my sister alone with their son time and time again? I will tell you one thing, my husband, Duane, is sitting over there in the gallery and we have five children together and if he felt any one of our children was a danger to me or anyone else, he would be around to protect me and get our child the right kind of help."

"Your Honor, my sister loved Dawson. She knew he was sick. And I believe from the depths of my soul that when Dawson was killing his mother, she was forgiving him. Katy was the most compassionate person I knew."

"Your Honor, Dawson needs help. He is

mentally ill and requires professional care. Please do not send him to prison. Please send him to a mental health facility. Katy would not want her son to go to prison for the rest of his life. Thank you for allowing me to speak today."

I walked away from the podium with my head held high and did not look at Tim, but into the eyes of my husband. I sat next to Duane and he grabbed my hand and held it tight. He whispered in my ear, "Katy is so proud of you right now. She is grateful for what you said here today. That took a lot of courage, Mary to stand up for Dawson."

Kathleen Karen

Katy, a sunlit halo bathes your face with our star's light,
Telling all what sweetness beheld you in terrestrial realms.
No mortal could have foreseen the ultimate sacrifice,
In future years, of your fierce motherly love.
Kathleen, meaning pure, a name so appropriately given,
Pushed into this world by a mother of the same name.
Your generous spirit, so freely given to all in need,
And taken without consequence by many.
My sister-friend, my heart that beat to the rhythm of yours,
As we whispered into long, dark nights of our youth.
Katy, my teacher, who taught me to mother by excellent example.
Our shared maternity clothes worn thin by constant use.
April 13th. I will forever celebrate the day God brought you,
     An angel to grace us with your true selfless love.

Hands in Namaskar, feeling peace, breath
radiates through my being.
Brain slows, finding release, body stretches
without seeing.
Downward dog, crow, half-moon, warrior,
triangle, and child's pose.
Receive calming strength soon, Shavasana
brings holy repose.
Yoga's gifts well received, for those who choose.
With practice, poses achieved cause body to
renew.
Reprieve from heart's ache, practice for my own
sake.

Sophia,
My Constant Companion

Sparkling Sapphire Sophia

Looking into your big eyes, I was smitten.
Body underweight, ribs showing, caused alarm.
Approached you slowly, so as not to be bitten.
Held you gently, protecting you from harm.
Brought you home, fed you well, gave you great care.
You grew to trust me; your young body grew strong.
Working around the house, you followed me everywhere.
Getting into mischief, figuring out right from wrong.
You became my constant companion, loyal friend.

When I was hurt, you comforted me.
This devotion, this love, you cannot pretend.
You opened my eyes to really see.
Time has changed your sleek body, not your mind.
Grateful for your gentle soul, so loving and kind.

Split Second

Slowly my eyes opened I squinted in the darkness of my bedroom, looking for the red digital numbers of my alarm clock. Finally, I spotted them and focused my eyes it read: 6:20 a.m. I had awakened before the alarm went off. What a relief. I detested that loud beeping noise that would have scared me awake at six-thirty. I stretched my legs and arms in opposing directions and rubbed the sleep from my eyes. I needed to wake up Sam for school. So I slowly pulled myself out of bed, grabbed my gold chenille robe from my bedpost, and wrapped it tightly around my shivering body. I walked over to my dresser and shut off the alarm clock with a click.

This morning was supposed to have a record low temperature of 23 degrees. I walked to the thermostat in the dark. It read 58, and so I turned it up to 66 degrees. I tiptoed out of my room so as not to wake Duane and closed the door silently. I flicked on the kitchen light and looked at the time on the microwave oven: 6:25 a.m. I started toward Sam's room when I heard a garbage truck's revving engine. "Darn it. We forgot to put the garbage and recycling out last night," I said, hoping someone would hear me. But I knew I was the only person awake, and I would have to do the chore myself.

I trotted back into the kitchen and pulled out the metal drawer on our trash compactor. I removed the plastic bag containing the garbage and clenched it at the top so the trash wouldn't spill on the floor. Again, I heard the garbage truck, sounding much closer this time. I ran with the garbage, my arms straining from the weight. I opened the front door, and the frigid air hit me like a wave of ice. I staggered down the steps to the front of the garage where the small black garbage container sat. I dropped the garbage in and closed the lid with a bang. I grabbed the garbage container and the blue recycling container by the handles and rolled them awkwardly down to the street and placed them two feet from the curb and three feet apart like the garbage company requires. I walked briskly back up the driveway and up the front porch steps into the house. What a relief to be in my warm cozy home.

I walked into the kitchen and removed the recycling container from the cabinet under the sink where we stored it and hobbled outside again, down the steps, down the driveway, and to the street. I emptied the contents and returned the same way. Again, I was happy to be in the warmth of my house. I could feel it heating up more since I had turned on the heater at 6:20 a.m. I went back into the kitchen and noticed that there were items to be recycled on the kitchen counter: a pink bakery donut box and a pile of newspapers. "Well, I might as well put those out, too," I said. I grabbed the box and papers and headed out the front door. I noticed it was 6:35 a.m. as I walked out of the kitchen.

I need to wake up Sam, I thought, but I walked out into the cold dark morning. The sun still had not risen on January 17, 2012, and it wouldn't for another hour.

Instead of walking down the driveway like before, I went down the front walkway because it was shorter. I was in my slippers on the concrete path when suddenly, my world turned upside down. In a split second, I slipped and lay on the cold, hard concrete trying to orient myself to what had just happened. My body was freezing, and I was shivering hard. The pink box and newspapers were strewn around my body. My left ankle throbbed in pain. I had slipped on ice, and there was no way I could put weight on my foot. I felt the bones click in my left ankle, and I was sure that I had broken it. I was so angry. My life had changed in a split second. All the yoga, walking, and swimming I had enjoyed would halt, and I would be stuck on the couch at home. I looked at my ankle again. It was so swollen, it looked like a huge log of bologna.

I lay in the dark, in my robe, with no one to help me. *How the heck am I going to get back in the house? There is no one here to help me."* Like *most things in life, I am going to have to get into the house by myself.* I forced myself to think of my next step. *Okay, my arms are not broken. I can use them.* I tested my right leg and flexed it. My right leg was okay, and I carefully turned myself over without letting my left foot touch the ground.

Okay, now I have to use my knees and

hands to crawl back into the house on my stomach. I started to crawl up the icy walkway, but I slid back down. "No," I cried. It was the shortest way back to the house. I had to try again. *I can do this.* I started to crawl with my hands and knees again. This time I used my fingernails in the cracks of the concrete and pulled myself along. I made it onto the part of the walkway that had no ice on it. "Thank you, God," I said out loud. I had gotten through the hardest part.

I slowly and methodically crawled up the 20-foot walkway and came to the front porch steps. *Oh my God. I thought I already did the hardest part. Boy was I wrong.* I had to turn my body over again so I could use my hands and bottom to scoot up the steps one at a time. I could only use my right foot though. *One step at a time.* I kept my left foot high without letting it touch the step. Finally, I got onto the flat part of the front porch. I continued to scoot on my bottom, using my hands to propel me along. I got to the front door and reached up with my left hand and open it. "Hallelujah," I yelled. The warm air enveloped me as I entered the house, and I began to feel safe.

My bedroom door was just to the right of the front door. I scootched in and slammed the front door with my right foot and reached up and opened the door to my bedroom. I could hear my husband breathing. I yelled, "Duane, I think I broke my ankle." No response. I scooted right next to the big bed and shrieked, "Duane, wake up. I think I broke my ankle."

I heard my husband move. "Mary, where are you?"

"I am on the floor." He bolted out of bed and ran around it and found me on the floor crying. He carefully pulled me up off the floor and helped me sit on the bed. "Mary, how the heck did you break your ankle?"

And I whimpered, "Well, Duane, it all started when I heard the garbage truck . . ."

New Beginnings

Reflections of the past, sadness seeping
like water through a sea sponge. Death,
tragedy, the unspeakable
Murder of my sister, Katy. Trying desperately
to cope.
Writing, meditation, yoga, walking to heal the
wounds of my heart.
Thoughts of my children, survival of my
husband, promise new life.
The flower of my spirit, struggling to touch the
light of the sun once again.

Colleen

Colleen is the firstborn child of my parents. She has always been a remarkable person. I was told by our mother that Colleen climbed out of her crib at one year of age to go to the bathroom. I have never seen, nor heard of any other child doing that. Mom said she worked hard to potty train Colleen because her second baby was due a few weeks after Colleen's first birthday.

Colleen grew up fast because our father was gone for six months at a time on an aircraft carrier while he was in the Navy. There is a joke in our family that every time Dad came home on leave, Mom got pregnant. It was partly true. Mom gave birth to seven children, but the last two babies, Mark, and I were conceived after Dad retired from the service.

Colleen has always had so much energy. She helped our mother take care of six children, cleaned house, and assisted in cooking. She was like a second mother to me. I don't remember her changing my diapers or carrying me around, but I was told that she did. Most of my memories are after we moved to Livermore when I was four years old. By that time, she was a sophomore in high school and hanging out with friends. I saw her mostly at the dinner table, where she always sat opposite our father at the other head of the table.

Colleen didn't care much for academics but excelled in typing and shorthand. She acquired a job at Concannon Winery after graduating from Livermore High School and worked in the office for eighteen years. I remember going on a tour there when I was six. I can still smell the pungent scent of wine fermenting in redwood barrels in the old brick winery. The air was a cool relief to the 100 plus degree heat of Livermore's summer. The office back then was a tiny stucco building that accommodated a couple of desks in the main space and had a small room in the back for Joe and Jim Concannon to conduct business.

Our parents respected Colleen. Mom was very close to her and depended constantly on her firstborn child. When I was sixteen, Colleen took over having Christmas Eve and Thanksgiving dinners at her home. From then on, it seemed that she was the matriarch of the family. Our mother suffered from anxiety and gladly gave up the chore of cooking for so many people. Colleen's table was always perfect with gleaming china, sparkling silverware, and lovely decorative centerpieces that represented the holiday we were celebrating.

I have always admired Colleen. She is an amazing cook and has a tastefully decorated home. She gardens, plants colorful annuals that line her front walkway, and mows her lawn. She can paint walls and assist with all kinds of projects from installing new windows to replacing toilets. She and Conley have remodeled their home to perfection.

While growing up, I felt inadequate around Colleen. Mom sang Colleen's praises while I listened patiently. As hard as I tried to gain our mother's approval, I could never measure up to my big sister. I realized in my thirties that Colleen would always be our mother's favorite daughter, so I let it go.

As the youngest of seven children, I tried my hardest to escape the role of being the baby of the family. I wanted to be taken seriously by my parents and siblings. Even after I gave birth to four children, I still was treated like the baby.

As the years ticked by, and we experienced the loss of our parents and three siblings, Colleen and I have become closer. Instead of being like a second mother, she is now my friend.

"Coll, we are the bookends in our family. Now, we only have Chris and Mark between us. You and I are the strong ones and always have been."

Colleen looked at me with tears in her eyes. "Yes, you are right, Mary. That's exactly what we are, bookends."

I almost lost Colleen when she was bitten by a tick while vacationing in Arkansas. Conley inherited his parent's home there. She was doing yard work and later that evening noticed a tick on her upper chest. Within a week, she thought she had the flu. By the time she came home, she was in bed and not getting up. I went to see her, and I knew immediately that she needed to go to the doctor. I told her husband, "Coll needs to go to the hospital. I am worried about her."

He waited three days. When he finally took her to the ER, she was going into organ failure. She was in the hospital for a week. The doctor told her, "Colleen, if you had waited one more day to get here, you would have died."

The doctor sent the tick to be tested for various diseases, but they never found the cause of Colleen's reaction. I am grateful she is still with me here on this earth. I couldn't imagine losing a third sister.

I gave Colleen a copy of my book for Christmas. I was excited for her to read it, hoping with all my heart she would like it. She had a cold on Christmas Eve but still amazingly had us over for dinner. Her house was a picture of perfection and her dinner, delicious as always. I called to check on her before I drove up to the cabin, and she didn't sound well. I said, "Colleen, please go to the doctors if you feel really bad. The weekend is coming up, and I don't want you to end up in the hospital."

"Okay Mare, I will go to the doctor if I feel worse."

We do not have Wi-Fi or phone at our cabin, and there is no cell reception. So, I thought of my sister for those few days I was away.

Three days later, Duane drove us home from the cabin. In an hour we were in cellphone range. I noticed Colleen had emailed me, and this is what she wrote:

Mary, I just wanted you to know that I spent the afternoon cuddled up in a big chair and blanket, reading your book. I'm impressed with your accomplishment of writing your first book and enjoyed it so much. It made me cry when I finished. Mom would have loved it! Love, Big Sis

I felt a warm glow begin in my heart and pass through the rest of my body. I finally had the approval and respect from my Big Sis. I am officially a grown-up.

Mark's Angel

A balmy breeze caressed my brother's face as he drove his silver GMC truck up Vista Boulevard to his home several miles from the Vista Grille Restaurant in Sparks, Nevada, which he has owned and managed for the last twelve years. The night before, he had gone to see a Don Henley concert with his daughter, Megan, who had recently found out she was pregnant. My brother was ecstatic about becoming a grandfather for the first time.

Mark joined his friends, Tim and Sarah, at the concert. Megan went home after the performance because she was tired from her pregnancy. Mark, Tim, and Sarah stayed out late having a few drinks and gambling at one of the local bars. They dropped Mark off at the Vista Grille on the morning of June 29, 2011, around 2:00 a.m. Mark decided to sleep at the restaurant before going home. After a few hours of sleep, he got into his truck, which was parked in the lot behind his restaurant. He only needed to drive four miles home.

He turned the key to start the ignition, rolled down his windows, and turned up the radio. The coral blush of the rising sun was visible in his rearview mirror.

He was used to late nights because he had been in the restaurant business since he was sixteen years old. He started as a dishwasher for the Old Livermore Railroad Restaurant in Livermore, California, in 1977, quickly working his way to a cook. Now, at the age of fifty, he had worked at many restaurants over the years: several of The Big Yellow House Restaurants, Sizzler, Sheraton, and Texas Roadhouse, to name a few.

He became a manager of the Big Yellow House in Milpitas at the age of twenty-one. Most of the restaurants served only dinner, requiring him to open the place at noon to let the prep cooks in and work until midnight or later, until the servers, bussers, and cooks finished the cleanup. As manager, he had to balance the books and count and deposit the money. My brother was a night owl, which suited his profession well.

As the sky turned from pink to orange, Mark's eyes got heavy. But it was only two more miles. He felt relaxed, reveling in the fun night he had with his daughter and friends at the concert. He was a huge fan of the Eagles, a popular rock group of the 70s. Don Henley, a former member, was having a great solo career, after the breakup of the band.

The sky turned pale blue. The two-lane road Mark was driving curved to the right and a median separated the two other lanes going the opposite direction back to Interstate 80. Mark's lids were heavy. His head tilted forward, and he dozed off. In a split second, his front left tire hit the concrete median bumping him awake. He overcorrected, turning the steering wheel to the right too fast. He lost control of the truck and careened into a ditch off the right shoulder of the road. The front of the vehicle slammed six feet down the gulley and hit a sandy dirt berm. The back of the truck flipped up and ejected Mark from the vehicle with a forceful trajectory. The truck stopped in a vertical position, the front bumper wedged into the dirt, and the back taillights shined up to heaven. My brother had been thrown twenty feet, lying unconscious, with his face down in the dirt, and bleeding in the scrub brush.

Mark hadn't noticed a car following a safe distance behind him as he drove on Vista Boulevard. A woman in a Nissan Sentra had seen the GMC truck in front of her weave a bit and wondered if the person driving was drunk or sleepy. When Mark hit the curb, she slammed on her brakes and watched in horror as he shot across the road in front of her and off the road, flipping to a vertical position. She immediately pulled onto the shoulder of the road and called 911 and reported the accident to the dispatcher giving the location and the need for emergency personnel as soon as possible.

After ending the call with the dispatcher, the witness unhooked her seatbelt, pushed on her hazard lights, ran to the crash site, and looked into the cab of the truck. The windshield had blown out, as well as the driver's side window. No one was in the vehicle. She trudged up the hill, the sandy dirt spilling into her shoes, scratching her Achille's tendons. She searched for a body. She found my brother, face down on the ground, blood spilling from his head and his mouth and his nose inhaling dirt. She had always heard not to move a body after an accident, but she could see the guy couldn't breathe. The woman sprinted to my brother, squatted down, and very carefully turned his head to the left, freeing his mouth and nose to breathe air. Her stomach turned when she saw the jagged wound across his forehead and his ear flopped at a strange angle. His left eyelid was cut open and swollen. His eye bulged out of its socket.

In the distance, she heard sirens and thanked God that help was on the way. His breath was shallow and gurgling. She stayed with Mark and prayed he would make it.

The fire truck and ambulance pulled over behind her car. The firefighters and EMTs ran up the hill where the woman waved her arms. When they got to Mark, they assessed his condition. As one of the EMTs reached my brother, he recognized him because he was a regular at my brother's restaurant. Using a stethoscope, the EMT, listened to my brother's lungs and said, "His left lung has collapsed. I have to insert a chest tube." The other EMT handed his partner the necessary equipment. The EMT put Mark's eye back in its socket.

The woman said to the workers, "I've always been told not to move a body, but I had to turn his head to the side. He couldn't breathe."

"Lady, you did the right thing, you saved his life."

The woman couldn't do anything more so she walked back to her car, shaken from the experience.

This woman who helped my brother didn't give her name to the emergency workers. She didn't help him to get her name in the papers. She aided another human being. I will forever call her my brother's angel.

Dream Dress

Mary, Halloween, 2013

W hen I was a little girl, I loved watching the Miss America Pageant. My favorite part of the show was when the young women glided elegantly onto the stage in their evening gowns. I especially admired the sparkling sequins gowns. *One day, when I grow up, I want to get a beautiful dress like that.*

That day arrived when I was thirty-one years old. Prior to that, I had been pregnant or nursing three of my children for the last eight years. I wasn't into the sexy dress mode during that period. It just wasn't practical.

When my youngest was two, my first

husband and I were invited to a Firefighters Valentine's Ball. I didn't have a formal dress to wear, so I went shopping at NewPark Mall in Newark. I walked around the mall, going into every store. Nothing. Then I entered Gantos clothing store, which sold women's formal wear. I didn't have to look long before a dress beckoned me, its shiny magenta sequins casting sparkles into my adoring eyes. I walked quickly over to the dress displayed on a mannequin. *Oh, please let it be my size.* I grabbed the tag and sure enough, it was.

A salesgirl saw me and asked, "Can I help you, miss?"

"Yes, please. I would like to try on this dress." I caressed the glittering sequins.

The young woman carefully took the dress off the mannequin and handed it to me. I was so excited. I rushed into the dressing room and threw off my clothes. I hurriedly put on the dress. I was almost afraid to look at my reflection for fear that the style would not be right for my body. I wanted this dress badly. When I turned around to view myself, I let out a squeal of delight. It fit me perfectly. The style of the dress was conservative in that it did not show any cleavage and covered my entire chest. It had a two-inch standing collar around my neck. The sexiness of the dress was created by the clingy fabric with its sequins expertly sewn on. It was sleeveless and had a slit that ended just above my knee.

I walked out of the dressing room to look at

myself in the three-way mirror outside the changing area. I was looking at the back of the dress when the salesgirl came over and said, "Wow, you look just like Jessica Rabbit. That dress was made for you. It's your lucky day because it's on sale. It's normally a $300 dress, but it is marked down to $100."

A huge grin spread across my face. It was my lucky day. The dress was going to be mine. I purchased the gown. I couldn't wait to show Mateo when I got home. I tried it on and excitedly walked out to our living room to show him. All he said was, "Don't you think it's a bit much?" Then he continued to read the paper. I was crushed. *What the hell is wrong with him?*

I have worn the dress a total of six times: three to balls, twice to captain's dinners on cruise ships, and to a Halloween party last year. I decided to dress up as Marilyn Monroe from the movie, *Some Like it Hot.* That's the funny movie with Jack Lemmon and Tony Curtis, who dressed up like women.

I was fifty-one at the time and thought I might as well wear it while I can still pull it off. I bought a platinum blonde wig, silver satin gloves, silver heels, and I wore my mom's silver fox faux fur coat. I was channeling Marilyn and felt like a million bucks.

When I showed up at the party, everyone complimented me on my costume. I love Halloween because I like pretending to be someone else for one night of the year. I chatted happily with friends and danced up a storm. It was the first time I had worn heels since I broke my left ankle two years before. The shoes were the only high heels I didn't give away because they were so comfortable, only two inches high.

I had several drinks at the party and as a result. I had to use the bathroom later that evening. I entered the bathroom, which glowed eerily from the two skull candles on the counter. I shut and locked the door and began lifting my dress so I could pull down my Spanx. While I was attempting this maneuver, I fell off balance into my friend's bathtub! I was laughing so hard I couldn't breathe until I tried to get out of the tub and couldn't. I had locked the door and the music was so loud from the party, no one was going to hear me yell for help. I certainly didn't want anyone to see me in this condition, in a tub with my Spanx down to my knees and dress pulled up to my waist. My legs hung out of the tub. I tried to hoist myself out with the strength of my arms, but I couldn't do it.

"Mary, how the hell are you going to get out of this mess?" I said out loud. I was sitting on the shower curtain, so I pulled on that to get some leverage and when I did, the shower pole and the rest of the curtain came crashing down on me. "Oh, no, this is just great. Think, Mary."

Coming up with a solution wasn't so easy after a few cocktails, but the pole crashing down on me sobered me up a bit. I used my right foot to push one shoe off. Once I did that, I used my bare foot to push off my other shoe. I pushed my Spanx down to my ankles and pulled it off so I could move my legs. Then, I threw them against the door. I lifted my legs over the edge into the tub. Then, I carefully stood up in the tub, trying not to fall again because of the slippery shower curtain and the pole that was in my way. Once I stepped out of the tub, I reassembled my outfit. I tried to put up the shower curtain and pole, but it kept falling, so I left it.

I exited the bathroom in search of my husband to help me. I told him the entire story. He laughed hysterically. "Okay, Duane," I said. That's enough. I am so embarrassed. Please go in the bathroom and fix the pole for me."

"Okay, Mary. I'll do it."

He came back in a few minutes and said, "It looks like someone else beat me to it. The shower curtain and pole are fixed."

"Duane, please don't tell anyone what happened to me."

"Mary, I will keep your secret to the grave."

The following Saturday, my sister Colleen invited us over for dinner. While we were eating, Duane told Colleen and her husband my embarrassing story, and we all laughed with tears in our eyes. So much for Duane taking my secret to the grave.

Vermillion Valley Resort

A h, Vermillion Valley Resort. When I first heard this name, I imagined a vast meadow of brilliant scarlet flowers shimmering in the noonday sun among viridian grass next to a sparkling azure lake surrounded by conifers of various species.

I was partly right. There were many kinds of trees at the resort, but the rest of my imaginings were far from correct. I was disappointed when I arrived and viewed the area. The lake had dried up, and there were no flowers in sight. I believe my arduous journey to get to the resort had much to do with my negative observations but let me digress.

I first heard of Vermillion Valley Resort or VVR, as experienced backpackers call it, from Duane. For the last year, he had been planning to hike the John Muir Trail in Northern California. This famous trail was named after the Scottish environmentalist, John Muir, who spent many years exploring the Sierra Nevada Mountains journaling and sketching plants and animals of the surrounding area. The trail begins in Yosemite National Park, goes through Kings Canyon Park, and ends in Sequoia National Park. The hike is approximately 210 miles in length with an elevation varying mostly from 8,000 to 11, 000 feet and up to 14,505 feet at the peak of Mount Whitney.

The JMT, as it is called by backpackers, had been on Duane's bucket list for quite a while. He is a cancer survivor and was first diagnosed ten years ago. I surmise that completing the JMT is Duane's way of feeling vibrantly alive and telling the cancer in his body to literally take a hike. Craig, our neighbor, was Duane's hiking partner for the trip. Craig's daughter, Bree, also joined them, as well as our daughter, Jill, and her husband.

Duane asked me, "Hey, do you think you and Julia can drive to VVR and bring us a resupply of food?" Julia is Craig's wife.

"Well, maybe. Where's that?" I asked.

"Oh, it's east of Madera," Duane replied.

"Where's Madera?" I asked.

"It's north of Fresno. By the way, Amando and Jamie are only hiking a week, so they need a ride home from VVR."

"Well, I guess so," I said hesitantly.

"We can stay in a hotel room or a yurt at VVR," he said, smiling.

"I've never stayed in a yurt. That sounds fun. Is it made of goatskin?"

"No," he said, laughing. "Here, look, there's a photo on the website." I looked at the photo, and the yurt looked comfortable with a proper bed and a little kitchen.

"Wow, that is not what I expected. It looks very cozy. Let's do it!" Little did I know what I was getting myself into.

Several months went by and Duane was furiously getting ready for his trip and buying expensive hiking equipment. My house was becoming increasingly cluttered with freeze-dried food, bear canisters, sleeping bags, backpacks, and tents. Jill and Gabe ended up staying in our house for six weeks before the trip because they were relocating to Southern California after the hike.

The week before they left, I had enough of the mess and talk about water filters and Jetboil stoves. My house looked like our local mountaineering store. Duane left for the trail on August 8, and Jill and Gabe left the next day. I breathed a huge sigh of relief. I finally had some peace and quiet, and I could get my house back in order. For the next three days, I scrubbed, vacuumed, and dusted to ready my house for Sandi's visit with her two aunts from Liverpool, England. They stayed with me for five days.

August 15, Julia and I packed up the resupply of food for our crew of hikers and took off for VVR. I confidently told Julia that I had gotten my printed directions off the internet, and that I was an experienced navigator. We arrived two hours later in Madera, right on schedule. We had lunch at Subway, got gas, and hit the road once more. The land became hillier, and then mountainous with pine trees appearing. We saw the signs for Huntington Lake, which my directions said VVR was, and we were so happy to be almost there around 2:30 p.m. We drove in a circle around the lake looking for VVR with no sign of it. I said, "Let's stop at the store and ask for help." We stopped, and I asked the storekeeper, "Can you please tell us where VVR is?"

"Oh, you poor people. They need to change the information on their website. The address you have is their mailing address. They are located 25 miles away, up in the mountains. You take the Kaiser Pass Road exit. It's a very bumpy, one-lane road. It will take you at least an hour to get there, if you're lucky," she said apologetically

"Really?" I said, stunned. "Well, okay thank you."

Julia and I got in the car and after we drove a few miles, we found Kaiser Pass Road. We drove about five miles farther and the road narrowed, getting very steep. Julia and I were both getting nervous. She could only drive five to ten miles per hour. After several more miles, we came upon a car heading the opposite direction, and because they were coming down the mountain, they had the right of way. So Julia had to back up and find a part of the road wide enough for the other car to pass. I had to get out of the car and help direct her. The granite cliff drop-offs were terrifying to look over.

We gave each other moral support by cursing the mountain, the road, and our husbands for making us drive this horrible road. At 5:30 p.m. we finally saw the small wooden sign for VVR. Ironically, Julia's phone rang at the same time. She put it on speaker. "Julia, where are you guys? Are you okay" Craig said with concern. They had expected us at 2:00 p.m.

"We're okay. We just saw the sign for VVR. We'll see you in a couple of minutes."

"Did you guys get lost?" he asked.

"Well, kind of. We'll tell you all about it when we see you," she said tiredly.

We walked into the VVR store, and Duane came up and gave me a bear hug. "Mary, I am so happy to see you." And then I realized how much I had missed my husband and why I drove all those miles. It was wonderful to see his joyful face and how much it meant to him that I had come.

If you go to VVR, I suggest you hire someone to take you there by helicopter. It will save you from getting many gray hairs and heart palpitations.

Duane Robert Heaton

Mary and Duane, July 8, 1995

I met Duane in March of 1994, at Sh-Booms, a dance club in Pleasanton. It took him two months, but he finally asked me out on May 12. Eight months later, we were married. Yes, it was a whirlwind courtship. Our friends and families didn't know what hit them.

I have celebrated many birthdays with Duane. How can that be? Time. It's such a mysterious process, sometimes flowing like wild honey or as blurry as bumblebee wings. I may not understand the secret of time, but I do know my relationship with Duane has been a remarkable experience.

We have shared so much joy: our wedding, with four of our children in attendance, the birth of our son, Sam, trips to Hawaii, Italy, and Ireland. Many graduations of our children. And let's not forget all the important everyday stuff: going for walks, dancing, laughing, playing Scrabble, going to the movies, and eating delicious food at our favorite restaurants.

The reality of life is the Yin and Yang. So, we have also shared sorrow, the loss of five members of my family and his stepsister, and then there was Duane's cancer battle. When I found out Duane was in stage four, I wasn't sure if he was going to make it. I felt lost, but miraculously he survived.

I cannot fully express how fortunate I feel that he is alive. He has been an inspiration to me. He has shown me how to be a positive person, always moving forward, living life to the fullest. Thank goodness Duane and I have had each other for support. He has been my rock on many occasions. I don't know what I would have done without him.

I am so proud of Duane. He has fulfilled many of his dreams: hiking the John Muir trail, walking Jill, his daughter, down the aisle, and seeing his youngest child, Sam, fly solo in an airplane before he graduated from high school.

And since Duane has checked these experiences off his bucket list, he has made another list: to retire with thirty-five years of service at UPS, walk the West Highland Way in Scotland, and to meet his first grandchild.

Duane retired on April 5, 2015, and looks forward to traveling across Europe, golfing, and enjoying all the pleasures life has to offer. But most of all, he wants to live with me in a beautiful place with lots of trees, a lake, and fresh air. I am looking forward to sharing this new chapter with him. Duane has been a loving and devoted partner for twenty-four years. I feel so blessed that he came into my life.

Changes

I am moving away from Livermore, a town where I have lived for most of my life. A town whose streets are etched in my brain like an internal landscape. Whose schools I have attended and my children after me. Livermore, a place of comfort to me for decades.

Leaving the physical place, that's the easy part. How am I going to live without my friends I have made throughout the years? Live without their comforting words which helped me through dark days and sleepless nights? I know it is the people I leave behind that make my move to another place so difficult. Once I tell my friends I'm moving, something shifts. They begin to guard themselves and so do I.

I want to tell all my friends I have met in this place of my childhood, adolescence, and adulthood that I cherish you, and my life is enriched by having known you. I will carry your love, support, and knowledge that you have given me to my next place of existence. I will not forget you and your kindness. I will look forward to emails, visits, and Facebook updates of how your lives evolve.

I will continue to be involved in your lives as much as I can from a distance. I will only live two hours and fifteen minutes away in a beautiful place called Lake of the Pines. It is on the way to Lake Tahoe and Reno, places many of you visit often. I will be a short drive from Interstate 80. Please come to see me.

I will also come back to Livermore to visit you as well as my sister, Colleen, who I have not told yet I am moving. I have tried to let her know, but I want to do it in person, and she has been too busy to see me. She only lives a mile away, but I see her maybe every two months because she is so busy with work. When she finds out I am moving, she will be upset, but maybe she will appreciate me more when I live 140 miles away. Ah, family. It can be so complicated.

I have told all five of my children. They were fine with the move. Jill, Alana, Amando, and Colton are adults living their own busy lives. It will not affect them much, but Sam is another story. I told him the news the other night and he said, "I am not ready to be independent, Mom."

"Sam, you can come with Dad and me. There will be room. There are two airports, one in Auburn and one in Grass Valley. You can continue to be a pilot. There is plenty for you to do up there. You can also attend Sierra College. But if you don't want to live with us, we can rent you a room in Livermore."

"I have to think about it, Mom."

Life is full of change. I tend to avoid it, but most of the time it happens anyway. I am trying to look at this as a new chapter of my life—an adventure. I have tried to calm my mind and body, but it has been challenging. I hope you all understand that moving is a necessity. I concluded that I do not want to have roommates in my beautiful Victorian home and so I am letting it go. It has been a wonderful place to live for the last eight years. It was my dream home, and I am fortunate I experienced living in it because only a few people can say that. Thank you all for your wonderful gift of friendship. I love you all.

A Day on the Lake

I t was another gorgeous spring day at the end of May in Lake of the Pines or LOP, as we call it. LOP is a community north of Auburn that my husband, Duane, and I moved to three months ago. Sam, our youngest child, had moved up the previous week, after finishing his first year of college at Las Positas in Livermore. Our friends, Teri, Charlie, and their son, Brandon, had invited us to an evening of boating on the lake. We accepted, grateful for their generosity. They are also the ones who introduced us to LOP.

Teri was working that day, so I offered to bring the food for the outing—deli sandwiches that I would make at home as well as fruit, chips and dips, and cold drinks—root beer and champagne. I assembled the sandwiches with ham, pastrami, turkey, Colby-Jack cheese, lettuce, tomatoes, mayo, and mustard on sourdough rolls. I tried to recreate a Togo's, which makes the best tasting sandwiches as far as I am concerned. Unfortunately, Teri and I are both gluten intolerant, so we had to abstain from the sandwiches.

We put on our swimsuits and packed the food, towels, sunscreen, and life jackets into our Jeep. We were ready to have some fun. We met Charlie and Brandon at the marina, a mile from our house. Sam, Duane, and Brandon helped negotiate the vintage turquoise and white ski boat into the lake while Charlie backed the trailer into the water with his truck.

Once the boat was successfully launched, we loaded our small ice chest and beach towels into the boat. Charlie warmed up the engine while we waited patiently. Another boat circled out away from us when the driver finally yelled, "Are you almost done? We are trying to dock our boat."

"Oh, yeah, sorry. I didn't see you out there," Charlie yelled back. He then put the boat into reverse, backed away from the dock, and proceeded forward, moving slowly out of the five-miles-per-hour zone.

Once we were out of the "no wake zone," Charlie revved the engine, and we shot through the water, the spray, misting my hot skin. It was four-thirty in the afternoon and 95 degrees. Teri would join us in a couple of hours after she got off work.

Charlie had brought a red and yellow covered inner tube. Brandon took the first turn. It was fun to see him being pulled through the water with a big smile on his face as he bounced on the tube. When Charlie made the first hard turn, Brandon bumped over the wake, shooting in an arc at a high velocity of speed on the water. Brandon screamed with glee as he catapulted in a right angle behind the boat and hung on for dear life. After several turns around the lake, Brandon was fatigued and let go of the tube. My arm shot up with the red flag to alert any other boats nearby that a person was in the water.

We motored over to Brandon and picked him up. He climbed into the craft. Then it was Sam's turn on the tube. He jumped into the water and shimmied up on the tube and yelled, "Hit it." Charlie gunned the motor, and the tube began to plane on the water.

I was experiencing a different feeling as my son bounced on the water. Those protective mother bear instincts surfaced as my son shot across the water while Charlie turned the boat. As Sam skipped across the wakes, bouncing and bumping, gripping the handles and screaming, as they say, "like a girl," I felt panic rise from my belly.

I was relieved when Sam held fast and didn't fly off the tube. My heart slowed to its normal rate, and I breathed again. Until the next turn. When Sam finally tired and let go of the flotation device, I was relieved until it was Duane's turn. My fear cranked up several notches as I watched my fifty-eight-year-old husband fly across the water. *He is getting too old for this.*

After we picked up Duane in one piece, thank God, Charlie said it was time to go back to the marina and pick up Teri.

When we arrived at the aluminum and fiberglass dock, I said, "Duane, I have to go to the restroom."

"Okay. Can you get my cell phone out of the glove box so I can take photos of us on the boat?"

"Sure." I grabbed the keys and climbed out

of the boat onto the shiny dock. I went to the restroom first, setting the keys on the shelf under the mirror. I washed my hands and picked up the keys and headed to the Jeep. I unlocked the glove box and grabbed Duane's black Samsung phone. I saw that Teri had arrived and was standing on the dock next to the boat.

I walked up to Teri and gave her a hug. I carefully handed Duane his cell phone as he sat in the boat. He took the phone and placed it on the dash behind the windshield. I then reached my hand out with the keys. When he reached for the keys, our hands hit each other. The keys dropped through a three-inch gap between the boat and the dock. It happened so quickly, there was no way either one of us could have caught the keys.

I looked down and then abruptly up and said to Duane, "Oh, shit." Both the car and house keys were on the ring.

He looked at me and shook his head. "Mary, you should have been more careful."

"I was being careful, but our hands hit. It just happened. It was an accident. This water can't be that deep. Maybe you can dive in and get the keys?"

"Yeah, I guess that is what I'll try to do." Duane climbed out of the boat and walked down the dock to the shore. He waded into the water along the edge of the dock and dived between the boat and the dock where the keys had fallen.

Duane's head popped up after the first

attempt. "It is pitch black down there. I can't see a thing, and my feet are in four inches of mud." He dived repeatedly trying to find the keys. After at least ten dives, I said, "Duane, why don't you let Sam and Brandon give it a try?"

"Okay," Duane said, but he kept going underwater. After he surfaced again, I repeated myself.

Finally, he let Sam and Brandon continue the search, but the keys were not to be found. After valiant efforts by all three, I said, "Let's go out on the boat and have some fun. Teri hasn't been out yet. We'll find the keys later. Maybe the security guy that patrols the lake can help us when we get back."

Everyone concurred and boarded the boat. Charlie started the engine, and we pulled away from the dock. We ate the snacks and sandwiches and drank root beer and champagne. We talked about how careful we must be with keys and cell phones around water. Brandon suggested getting a foam floaty to attach to our keys, which was a good idea. Sam brought up that having cell phones on boats was an accident waiting to happen, and that getting a waterproof case would be worth the purchase.

Brandon wanted to try to water ski so he jumped out of the boat, and Duane handed him each ski. Brandon had a difficult time putting them on but finally was able to do it. He made several attempts to ski and after the fifth, he was on the water for about five seconds before he lost his grip. When we motored over to him, he said, "I am too tired to try anymore. I'm done for today."

No one else wanted to use the skis or tube, so Charlie drove slowly around the lake. I enjoyed looking at the beautiful homes around the perimeter with their manicured gardens. It was a lovely evening, and I forgot about the lost keys for a while.

We headed back to the dock and by a stroke of luck, the lake patrolman was on the dock. I went to the restroom and when I came back, the man was talking to Duane.

"If I were you, I would get a garden rake, a rigid one, and come back later to get your keys. They aren't going anywhere."

"That is a good idea. I think I will do that tonight," Duane said.

While Duane and the man talked, Teri listened to the conversation a few feet away at the end of the dock. I saw that she had her cell phone in her hand. Suddenly, her phone dropped, hit the aluminum dock, and slid with lightning speed into the water.

"Oh, shit!" Teri said. "My cell phone just fell in the lake."

The patrol guy turned around, looked at her, and walked away without another word.

I saw the entire scene and stifled a giggle. It was so ironic. After all the talk about being careful and trying to prevent accidents, it happened again.

Teri investigated the water. "I can see my

phone. Come here. Look you guys. There it is."

Brandon dived in and retrieved her phone. He said, "Mom, you have to put it in rice right away."

"I will son. Thanks for getting it for me."

We all laughed about the events of the evening and headed home. Duane and Sam helped unload our stuff but then got a flashlight and a rake to go find our keys. They came back a half hour later, smiling. "Mom, we found the keys. The rake worked."

"That's awesome, Sam. Shit happens, but things always seem to work themselves out."

Susan Elaine Wilson

Susan Elaine Wilson

S usan Elaine Wilson: Poet, teacher, spirit guide, healer, and friend. I was stunned when I received an email from Flora, my former classmate, sharing the sad news of Susan's death. Susan was too young to die; she was timeless.

My first impulse was to contact the other women who shared a safe space for a matter of several years, who could share the grief I was feeling. Susan brought us together and we shared laughter and tears and listened to each other with compassionate hearts.

I was guided to Susan in an interesting way. I was teaching at Valley Montessori School in Livermore. I taught a joyous girl named Jacqueline. At the end of the school year in

2006, her mother, Terry, gave me a generous gift, a certificate for a massage. Terry owned the Three Palms Day Spa.

Terry and I graduated in the same class at Livermore High in 1980. I called her to make an appointment. She informed me she employed three massage therapists. She said, "Mary, I know exactly which therapist I would choose for you, Susan Wilson.

I trusted Terry and booked the appointment.

When I met Susan for the first time I knew Terry had chosen the right person for me. Susan and I got along well. It was extremely important for me to connect with a massage therapist because there needs to be a level of trust.

I continued seeing Susan every few months for a couple of years when she said "Hey, Mary, I am starting a writing class at my house. It is a group of women, and we are going to write from our personal experiences. It would be perfect for you because you are a born storyteller."

"Really? You think I am a storyteller? I never thought of myself as a writer. The last time I wrote anything was in college, and those were term papers."

"Every time you come to an appointment, you tell me stories of your life. Just write them down." Susan convinced me to join her class starting in June 2009.

As my first writing class with Susan I contemplated my oldest brother, Patrick, who was in San Joaquin Hospice, dying from

Parkinson's disease. He was only fifty-five years old. It was extremely sad. The disease had ravaged his body. I visited him every couple of days. The nurses told us he was getting close to death.

I had just arrived home from the hospice center on June 16th when my sister, Katy, called me. She said, "Mary, Pat just passed away."

"I am grateful you were there when Pat passed. I am glad he did not die alone." I hung up the phone and sat there crying. I had just left him forty-five minutes earlier. I had sung to him and hopefully, I gave him some comfort.

My first writing class was to begin in a half hour. I sat there thinking, "Should I stay home and grieve for my brother or go to Susan's writing class?" I wasn't sure. I sat quietly as tears rolled down my cheeks. "What should I do?" Then a voice told me, "Mary, you need to go to the writing class. It will help you."

I listened to that voice. It was difficult, but I shared with Susan and my new classmates what had transpired an hour before. I did not know these women, but I felt very comforted. It was the safe place that I needed.

Three months went by, and I was going to class each week. This time my mother was in the same hospice, and she died on September 21, 2009. I went to class and shared that my mother had died. Writing about it helped me to cope with her passing.

I continued with the women's writing group

until Susan ended it. She suggested that I take her class at the Livermore Parks and Recreation Center. I signed up and went to class.

I met some amazing people, and it continued to be a safe place to express myself. Every Thursday, I couldn't wait to share what I wrote and listen to what my classmates were going to read that day. We became a close-knit group of mostly women and a few brave men. I hosted the first writer's luncheon at my house on Seventh Street and eventually, other writers followed suit. Our group became very social.

In October 2011, I received the shocking news. My sister Katy was dead, murdered by her son, Dawson. There were no words to express my naked grief. I called Susan and told her what had happened. I asked her permission to be the first reader at our Thursday class and asked if I could bring my husband. She gave me permission for both. She was very supportive of what I needed to do.

On Thursday, November 3, I went to class with a heavy heart. Susan let the class know that I had suffered a great loss and that I needed to read to them what happened to my sister. It was my first act to help start my grieving process.

As the months wore on, I continued to write stories. They gave purpose, strength, and meaning to my life. The next year when my nephew's trial began, I again needed an outlet for the quagmire of feelings that stirred in my soul.

I coped with my situation and began to write about a trip I took with my daughter to Ireland. A voice inside me told me to keep writing about it, and then it became a book. I never dreamed I could write a book, but I did.

Susan had a quiet way of instilling in me that I could accomplish anything. She gave me confidence, hope, and strength. I don't know what I would have done without her writing classes. They helped me process the deaths of three loved ones and the trial of my nephew.

Before I moved away, I met with Susan and gave her a gift that my brother, Pat, had given to me on my birthday, July 8th, which was also Susan's birthday. It was a porcelain rose. I gave it to her because it meant so much to me and because the first day of my writing class was the day Pat died. I wanted to demonstrate to Susan how much she changed my life for the better.

The Sound of Music

My earliest memory is of my mother's lovely soprano voice. She sang merrily around the house while doing housework. It always made me happy when I heard her sing. Mom loved to watch musicals on TV too. I sat with her on Saturday afternoons and watched old movies together.

One of Mom's favorites was *The Sound of Music,* which came out on April 1, 1965, just a few months before my third birthday. Mom purchased the album with the songs from the movie. We kids loved the fact we had the same number of children as the von Trapp Family and Captain von Trapp reminded us of our father and Maria reminded us of our mother with her beautiful voice and Catholic upbringing.

We had a stereo in the living room, and Colleen put on *The Sound of Music* album and we reenacted different scenes from the movie. One night when our parents were out to dinner, all seven of us took turns running down the staircase in our house belting out, "The hills are alive with the sound of music." It was such a delightful evening and one of the few times I remember all seven of us laughing, singing, and dancing together.

In December 1968, the musical *Hello Dolly* was playing at the Vine Theater in town, and Mom and Dad took us kids to see it. I absolutely loved the movie. Mom bought that album too. For my tenth birthday, Mom and Dad took me to see *Hello Dolly* at the Orpheum Theater in San Francisco, which was a very big deal for me because I had never been to a live musical.

Music has always held a very special place in my heart and so, at the age of eight, I took a music test given at Rincon Elementary at the beginning of the school year. Any child that was interested in playing an instrument was invited to take the test. I told my teacher, Mrs. Decker, that I wanted to take it. The students that scored the highest on the test got the instrument of their choice for free. Eight to nine-year-olds could choose to play a string instrument, so I chose the violin. I did not score the highest, although I did well on the test. I had to rent a violin from the music store in town. Sixth-grade students could play a woodwind, brass, or percussion instrument. I played the violin for two years. I liked it, but I had my sights on playing the flute.

As soon as I began sixth grade, I began taking flute lessons from Mrs. Wilhite. My class started with twelve flute players, but after two months, I was the only student left. Blowing into a flute is not an easy task and most girls did not have the knack for it. Some of the girls just lost interest and did not want to practice. So on Friday afternoons, I went to the music room and got private lessons from Mrs. Wilhite.

I continued playing flute once I entered Junction Avenue Middle School. I joined the concert band. Mr. Chambers was my teacher. I met my friend, Mary McLaughlin in band. She also played the flute. Mary and I had a lot of fun sitting next to each other.

I was in band through eighth grade, and at the end of the school year, Mary and I were asked to play in the pit band for the musical, *The Music Man.* We had to go to the rehearsals the last three weeks before opening night. We listened to the students sing the songs repeatedly, while we accompanied the actors. I knew every song by heart and the dialog too. I thought, if they need an understudy, I can say the words and sing all the songs of Marion, the lead role in the play. Unfortunately, I was too shy to sign up for drama in middle school, so I stuck with band.

I continued to play the flute through my freshman year at Livermore High. I enjoyed playing the flute, but my true love was singing.

My brother, Chris, was in his senior year, and he was in the two auditioned music groups, *a Capella* and Madrigals, at school. I wanted to sing in the a Capella group, but I had to audition, and I was terrified. Chris gave me a few pointers and let me know where the audition was located and I signed up.

I stayed late after school on Friday so I could go to my audition. I walked into the music room, and my heart pounded in my chest. My face was beet red because whenever I got nervous, my face flushed. I called it the Irish curse.

I said, "Hello, my name is Mary Hansen, and

I am here to audition for a Capella. Chris is in the choir now. He is also in Madrigals."

The choir director was a tall man with black hair, a bushy mustache, and a booming baritone voice. He said, "Hi, Mary. Chris told me you were going to audition. I am Mr. Heiner. What do you think, are you a soprano or an alto?"

"I am definitely a soprano. I sing high like my mother."

"Okay. These two other students and I are going to sing with you. We sing in four-part harmony in a Capella. Jenny will sing alto, John will sing tenor, and I will sing bass. We are going to sing a hymn out of this music book. Chris told me you play the flute, so you know how to read music. You need to sightread the notes and sing along, okay?"

"Okay," I said nervously.

"The hymn is called, 'Only Trust Him.'

I was sure going to have to trust Him because I had been raised Catholic and the song did not sound familiar to me. The two students picked up hymnals and Jenny handed me one and we all turned to song fifty-three. Mr. Heiner motioned to the piano player across the room, and she played the introduction to the song.

By this time, my face was crimson. *How the heck am I going to do this? I have never sight-read music and used my voice.* The three of them began to sing their parts, and I was lucky because sopranos sing the melody and that is what the piano player was emphasizing. I looked at the notes on the page and miraculously, I was able to sing along with them.

When we finished the song, Mr. Heiner said, "Mary, that was great sight-reading. You have a pretty voice. I will have a list of the new a Capella choir outside the music building next Monday morning. Thank you for coming in for the audition."

The entire weekend I kept thinking about whether I was going to get into a Capella. I was hoping with all my heart I would. If I did not make it, I could sign up for the mixed chorus that Mr. Heiner taught. I wanted so badly to be in a Capella because I heard them sing and they were so good.

I got up Monday morning with butterflies in my stomach and got ready for school. I raced my Schwinn ten-speed bike to school. I locked up my bike and walked quickly to the music building across the campus. I skipped up the steps, and I could see a sheet of paper taped to the door. I took a deep breath and scanned the paper for my name. I looked down the list and there it was, Mary Hansen. I was so happy and grinned from ear to ear. I had made it into a Capella.

I had a great sophomore year singing with a Capella. It was a group of eighty students and there were many talented singers. Our group was amazing, and we went to several music festivals and won awards. I met Cris Cassell at the Old Livermore Railway restaurant where we worked. I was very happy she was also in the choir. Cris had a lovely soprano voice.

There was one song we sang called "Saul." I will never forget when we performed it at the Mormon Temple in Oakland. It was a very powerful song in which Jesus is questioning Saul. The dynamics were extremely intense. I remember watching the audience nearly jump out of their seats when we sang the word Saul at triple fortissimo, which is the loudest we were taught to sing. It still gives me goosebumps when I think about that song.

I auditioned for the Madrigal group at the end of my sophomore year, and I made it. I was overjoyed. It was a group of twenty singers, five sopranos, altos, tenors, and basses. The absolute key to this choir was the blending of voices. It was imperative that we sounded like one voice in each singing section.

I loved singing in the Madrigal choir, but I had to be brave because I couldn't hide in such a small group. Fortunately, I had no vibrato and my voice blended perfectly with the other sopranos. One day during a rehearsal, Mr. Heiner said, "Mary, you have a perfect choir voice." I will never forget his words.

My favorite songs to sing in Madrigals were the Gregorian Chants written in Latin. We sang them with no musical accompaniment, only our twenty voices. Many of our concerts were held at St. Michael's Catholic Church in Livermore, which had the most amazing acoustics. Our Madrigal group positioned ourselves individually in each corner of the church and choir balcony. Our voices blended, soaring into the vaulted ceiling of the church. It was a breathtaking experience. I learned to sing in many different languages: Latin, German, French, Spanish, and Italian. Mr. Heiner taught me to read musical notation and how to correctly pronounce words. My three years in a Capella and Madrigals were priceless.

During college, I didn't have time for choir because it conflicted with my necessary classes. After I gave birth to Alana, Amando, and Colton, I sang to them all the time. I taught them many songs.

I joined the Ohlone Community Choir when I was twenty-eight years old. It felt so good to be singing with a group again. At thirty, I began taking a class at Ohlone College called Music for Minors. It was a class on how to teach music to children, and I enjoyed it.

I began volunteering at my children's elementary school at a time when the music programs had been taken out of the school curriculum. I was appalled when I heard that the students at Hirsh Elementary School would not have a music program, and I wasn't going to let that happen. I let the principal know that I would teach the children songs each week. I loved singing with the students, two of which happened to be my children.

After Duane and I were married in 1996, we moved to Livermore. I saw a job listing in the newspaper for a music teacher at Rancho Las Positas Elementary School. I applied and was interviewed. I was hired on the spot. I taught music to all 535 students at the school. I taught students from kindergarten to fifth grade, sixty kids at a time. I carried my Fender acoustic guitar from classroom to classroom. Alana, Amando, and Colton all attended the school. I was pregnant the second year I taught. I had minored in ASL in college. Sometimes I taught a song with American Sign Language and used CDs to accompany us while we sang. The holidays were especially fun, teaching Halloween and Christmas songs. I taught there for two years and then the funding ran out.

I had given birth to Sam and was busy raising five children. I eventually sang with the Las Positas Community Choir for a few years during this time and even sang in a rock band for a year. The musicians I sang with from work at Lawrence Livermore Laboratory. We called ourselves The Replaceable Units.

When we switched Sam to Valley Montessori and I became a teacher there, I got to sing every day with my students. I began my class each day with music. The children entered the classroom and joined me on the rug sitting in a circle and we sang seven songs. I played the guitar to accompany us. I taught at VMS for seven years.

When Pat was at the end stages of Parkinson's disease, he was transferred from a board and care facility to Hospice of San Joaquin where I sang to him. I felt it would bring him comfort. They say the last sense to go is hearing, so even though my brother couldn't see me, he could hear my voice. I wanted him to leave this world with the comforting sounds of music.

Three months later, I sang for my mother as she lay in the same hospice facility. I sang to bring her comfort. I could not help thinking how the tables had turned because she sang to me when I was a child.

I also sang at Peggy's, Pat's, and my mother's memorial services. I sang at my friends parents' memorial services. After Katy died, I sang "Let it Be" as we scattered her ashes in the San Francisco Bay. Music still soothes my soul and brings me comfort.

Two years after Katy died and my grief was lessening, I connected once again to the Hospice. I was told they had a small choir that sang to hospice patients, and so I began volunteering. I did that for a year and eventually began going out by myself to board and care facilities to sing to hospice patients. It was one of the most rewarding experiences I have ever had.

In 2018 I had Mark and Sandi's wedding at my home at Lake of the Pines. Once again, Cris Cassell and I got to sing together. We performed two songs, "To the Morning" by Dan Fogelberg and "Wildflowers" by Tom Petty. It was wonderful to sing for such a joyous occasion. All my family members and childhood friends were in attendance, and it was such a happy day.

Since I moved to Lake of the Pines, I have sung at a few memorial services for friends. I also sang for Keri, my friend Teri's mother. I sat with her and sang songs and spoke with her as she prepared to leave this earth. It was an honor to bring comfort to Keri. She passed away two days later. Music has brought me endless hours of joy and has gotten me through the most difficult times of my life. I don't know what I would do without the sound of music.

The Guitar

Mary and Sam playing his guitar

I bought my first guitar when I was fourteen with money I had saved. I signed up for guitar lessons at the Music Source on First Street in Livermore so I could learn properly.

I went to the guitar lessons during the summer of 1976, but I had to walk the two miles carrying my guitar in the summer heat, and it was exhausting. My parents only had one car and Dad drove it to work.

I enjoyed my lessons and practiced during the week, but the walking and heat got to be too much and I stopped going. My one consolation was that I still played the flute and had signed up for the concert band at Livermore High my freshman year. I got very busy with studying and practicing my flute for band, so the guitar I purchased sat in the closet.

The following year, Mark began taking

guitar lessons at Livermore High and he asked me if he could borrow my guitar and I said yes. The guitar eventually became Mark's, and he bought it from me for $50. I regret to this day that I did not continue to practice guitar when I was young.

In 1992, right before my thirtieth birthday, I decided I wanted to purchase myself a special gift to commemorate turning thirty, a guitar. I wanted a high-quality guitar and since I did not play, I felt I needed a person who played guitar well to come with me to pick it out. Mark was living in Idaho at the time, so I asked Pat if he would come with me to various guitar stores to help me choose a guitar.

I chose a Saturday in late June because Pat worked during the week. We went to San Jose to a few music stores. Pat played many guitars for me, but we didn't feel any was the right one. I lived in Fremont at the time, so I said, "Hey, Pat, there is a music store called Allegro Music in town. Why don't we go there? It is not a large store, but they do have guitars."

"Okay Mare, let's go."

We arrived at the store where many guitars hung on the walls. We had the store clerk take several of them down for us. Pat played a few of them. We were not impressed. Then he picked up a Fender folk acoustic and began to play "Blackbird," by the Beatles. I listened to the beautiful fingerpicking Pat played, and it sounded lovely, the tone pleasing to my ear and the sound resonated fully with each note. I just listened and did not say a word.

"Mary, this is the one. It plays well and has a great tone. This is your guitar," Pat said.

"I agree Pat. It has a beautiful tone. I could hear it as soon as you began to play. Thank you so much for coming with me and helping."

I went to find the clerk to let him know I would purchase the guitar. He rang it up and the cost was $225, plus tax, which was quite a bit of money, but I wanted a quality instrument.

I had taken the Music for Minors course at Ohlone College in Fremont and met a woman named Susan Stein who played guitar. I had heard she gave lessons. I called her and told her I wanted to take lessons. And so, at the age of thirty, I began the process of learning to play guitar once again.

I was able to play the basic chords after a few months and brought the guitar with me when I taught music to the children at Hirsh School. I was a novice, but the kids did not care.

After Duane and I got married in 1996, we moved to Livermore and I got a job as a music teacher at Rancho Las Positas Elementary School. It was the school Alana, Amando, and Colton attended. I was so excited to start singing with the children.

I taught music five mornings a week from 9:00 a.m.to noon. I carried my guitar from one classroom to another and played the songs I learned in Music for Minors, as well as songs I received from Susan. I loved being a music teacher. The students were always happy to see me. I was like their favorite aunt bringing them presents.

I began the following school term and found out I was pregnant in October. I continued to sing and play guitar for the children and they watched my belly grow with each month that went by. I was due on June 21st and wondered if I would make it through the entire school year. The last day of school was June 13th.

It was getting difficult to carry the guitar by the beginning of June. My belly was so big I could barely place my guitar on my knee to play. The baby inside seemed to react every time I played, dancing around inside my womb. It made me smile. Sometimes a student asked if he or she could touch my tummy. I said, "Sure."

June 13th, and it was the last day of school. I had made it through. We celebrated and I let the students choose their favorite songs and I played them. It was a very fun day.

The following week on June 18th, I went into labor. On June 19th, I gave birth to a nine-pound boy, and we named him Samuel Richard Duane Heaton. I played my guitar at home until I began teaching at Valley Montessori School in 2003. I began each day singing. It was a wonderful way to begin the day because it calmed the children.

I worked at VMS for seven years and continued to play guitar for my students. In 2010 I became very ill with an autoimmune disorder called Mastocytic Enterocolitis. My doctor told me I could not teach young children anymore, and she put me on disability. I was devastated, but it was important that I get well. I went to school and brought my guitar home. I pulled my guitar out and played it from time to time.

In 2016 Duane and I moved to Lake of the Pines and I brought my guitar along and continued to play it occasionally. A year later, I broke my left wrist. After I got the castoff, it was very difficult for me to play my guitar. The body of the guitar was quite large, and it was hard to stretch my left wrist around to play chords on the fretboard.

It made me feel sad when I looked at my guitar sitting in the closet and not being played. I asked each of my children if they wanted the guitar and each said no. I even asked again, and they still said no.

One day I was at a party, and my neighbor, Scott mentioned that he was looking for an acoustic guitar. He had gone to many stores and had not found the right one. He was also checking online.

I said, "Scott, I have a beautiful Fender folk acoustic guitar, and it is in great shape. I want you to look at it. Since I broke my wrist, I can't play it. An instrument should be played and not sit in a closet. I asked all my kids if they wanted it and they said no."

"Are you sure, Mary?'

"Yes, I am sure. Why don't you come over tomorrow and take it? Play it for a week and let me know if you want to buy it."

Scott came over the next day and I showed him the guitar. He opened the case and then picked up the guitar and strummed it.

"Wow, this guitar is in really good shape for how old it is."

"Yes, it is. I have taken good care of it. She is a beauty, huh?"

"She sure is. I will take her. How much do you want to sell her for?"

"I think $150 is fair, but you take her home and let me know. Think on it."

A week later Scott called me and said, "Mary we have a deal. I will bring over the $150 today."

"Sounds good, Scott. I am happy that you are buying my guitar. I am glad to be selling it to a friend."

A few months went by and Sam was living in Carmichael. He was attending Sacramento City College. He came home for a visit and brought a guitar with him. I said, "Sam, where did you get that guitar?"

"I am borrowing it from Kelly, Colton's girlfriend."

"Sam, I really wish you had told me because I sold my guitar to Scott."

"Oh, that's too bad."

I could hear Sam practice guitar in his room when he visited. As the weeks and months went by, he got better and better. His fingerpicking skills were excellent. I kept thinking, It is no wonder Sam plays so well he heard me playing guitar almost every day in the womb. I sure wish I hadn't sold my guitar.

December arrived and Duane and I were invited to a Christmas party at our friend, Deanne's, house. I saw Scott's wife Sherilyn and went over to chat with her. We caught up and then she said, "By the way, how is Sam doing? I haven't seen him in a long time."

"He is well. He is getting straight A's. He really loves his classes. By the way, he started playing guitar and he is amazingly good. He is borrowing a guitar from Colton's girlfriend."

I went on to tell her the story of my guitar, how Pat helped me choose it, and how I played it while Sam was growing inside of me.

"Mary, you know what that means, right? Scott needs to sell you back the guitar. Sam should have it."

"Sherilynn, really? It would mean so much to me to be able to give Sam that guitar. I wished he would have taken it up sooner. I feel so bad. I know how much Scott loves that guitar."

"It will be okay. Scott will get over it. Sam must have the guitar. It is rightfully his."

"Thank you so much for understanding. Please speak with Scott just to make sure, okay?"

"Okay. I will give you a call."

The next day Sherilynn called me and said, "Scott was disappointed, but he understands why it means so much to you to give the guitar to Sam."

"You both have made me very happy. I am going to give it to Sam for Christmas. It will be a big surprise."

On Christmas morning when Sam woke up, he came out to the family room, and there under the tree was my old guitar. I told him the story of how it made its way back into our family. He was so touched, his eyes glassy. I gave him a long hug.

Sam serenades us playing the guitar and even sings to us when no one else is around. He has a musical talent that a person is only born with. I love to hear him play. He has also played for Scott and Sherilyn, and it confirmed to them that they did the right thing by giving back the guitar.

Mary's first book

As I sat down to write about a life-changing event, I asked myself this question: What actions have I taken to change my life for the better? These are a few topics I have written about previously: motherhood, teaching, standing up to injustice, and my family. Then, I experienced a huge life changer. I wrote *Rambling Through the Emerald Isle* and had it published.

When I tell people I have written a book, they ask, "Have you always wanted to write a book? Was it a dream of yours?"

The answer is no. I started writing in 2009.

I didn't write before that, except in school. As a child, I was in the lowest reading and writing group. A few of my teachers told me I wasn't a good writer, so I believed them. It wasn't until I took a writing composition class at Livermore High with Mrs. Anne Homan that a teacher encouraged me to write. She asked us to write about a favorite tree.

For some reason, I couldn't wait to write about a tree. I went home and wrote about the magnolia tree in my front yard. I used descriptive words about the color, texture, and smell. To my astonishment, I got an A on my paper.

Mrs. Homan wrote a note on my essay that she enjoyed my description of the magnolia tree, and that I was a good writer. I felt elated. A teacher thought I wrote a good paper. It made me feel more confident about myself.

After I graduated from high school, I attended college and had to write many essays, but I didn't feel very inspired. Then, I took a creative writing class with Professor Williams, and it was a positive experience. We were required to read American short stories and had to write about them. For some reason, the exercise in writing about how I felt about a character inspired me.

After college, I got married and within several years had three young children. There was no time for writing. I did, however, spend a great deal of time reading books to my kids. I enjoyed going to the library with them choosing many books to read. I loved the picture books with beautiful illustrations. I still had my favorite children's books: *Where the Wild Things Are, Madeline,* and the *Cinderella Skeleton.* I read these books repeatedly to my children. It crossed my mind on occasion to write a children's book, but never a book for adults.

A few years later, I divorced, remarried, gained a stepdaughter, and had another child. I was an extremely busy mom cooking, cleaning, and driving the kids to and from school with little time for myself. When my youngest was in first grade, I went back to college to get my Montessori teaching credential.

While I loved teaching children ages three to six, it was exhausting. When I got home from work, I had very little energy for anything but the household chores. Again, there was little to no time for me or what I wanted to do.

A few months after I began teaching, my husband was diagnosed with cancer. Sam our youngest, was seven years old. It was a difficult time. I tried to keep it all together, but and it wasn't easy. I needed a creative outlet.

I started going to a massage therapist, Susan Wilson, to ease my stress. She heard me talk about my challenging life. She encouraged me to write my stories. It took a few years for her to convince me, but in June of 2009, I began taking her writing class. Pat died half an hour before the first class, and I decided to go anyway. It was one of the best decisions I have ever made. Being able to write my feelings opened a creative part of me that I had used so little.

I haven't stopped writing since that first class. I figured out that I had to write about the sadness first and after a while, I started to write about funny experiences. I just kept writing. Taking Susan's class was a wonderful motivator to keep writing. I realized that during our breaks from class, I didn't write, and that was not good. I felt calmer after writing a story. Now, I need to write, and it has become a positive habit.

Susan asked us students to write about a vacation experience. As soon as she mentioned the prompt, I knew I was going to write about flying to Ireland with my daughter. I wrote about the funny, yet terrifying, experience of driving on the wrong side of the road in Ireland. I read the story and my classmates laughed.

Susan gave us another writing prompt that day, but when I got home my inner voice kept saying, "Mary, you have to write the entire story about why you went to Ireland," so I did. I began writing the story in April of 2013 and finished by September. I asked my best friend, Sandi, to read my first draft, and she encouraged me to have it published. On January 1, 2014, I called her and said, "Sandi I will publish my book this year. It will be my goal."

I was determined to achieve my goal. I researched traditional publishing versus self-publishing. I found that I would have more freedom if I self-published a book, and I liked that aspect. But while I was reading about all the publishing companies, I was overwhelmed. Which one should I choose for my book?

While I was talking with some of my writing classmates about the challenges of choosing a publishing company, Lynda said, "Hey, Mary, I have the name of a woman who published my book, and now she is helping other new writers publish their books. Here are her name and phone number."

I thanked Lynda and called Paula Chinick at Russian Hill Press and met with her. It was nice having someone guide me through the publication process. She suggested an independent editor, interior formatter, and a book cover designer, who all helped me each step of the way. It took about 70 days to publish my book. There were a few challenges, but nothing I couldn't handle.

On December 6, 2014, I had a book signing party. The books were delivered by UPS, and when I opened the boxes to look at my printed books, I was overcome with a sense of joy, mixed with pride and accomplishment. I worked very hard to reach my goal, and now I am an author, and it feels exhilarating.

Autobiography of a
Good Girl

Jamie (daughter-in-law), Jill, Mary, Alana, and Kelly (Colton's girlfriend). Front row: Amando, Gabe (son-in-law), Duane, Sam, Tommy (Alana's boyfriend), and Colton.

Youngest of seven does what she's told, keeps peace in the household.

Feels invisible. Wants to feel love. Consolation comes from up above.

Tries to be noticed with good deeds, falls short, gets what she needs.

Forever responsible at work and school, goes above and beyond, life can be cruel.

Becomes a woman looking for fun, marries early, husband on the run.

Births many babies whom she adores, fills time with diapers and chores.

Finally finds love, enjoys life, makes a new home, is a good wife.

Becomes a teacher, shares love of learning.
Much responsibility causes yearning.
Nearing sixty opens her eyes. She sighs. Was
being good worth it?
She is not sure, but in her heart, knows the good
girl will never part.

CPSIA information can be obtained
at www.ICGtesting.com
Printed in the USA
LVHW012243130121
676362LV00006B/1228

9 781735 176369